D1365385

# AUDREY HEPBURN

# AUDREY HEPBURN

## A Biography

Martin Gitlin

GREENWOOD BIOGRAPHIES

GREENWOOD PRESS
WESTPORT, CONNECTICUT • LONDON

**Library of Congress Cataloging-in-Publication Data**

Gitlin, Marty.
  Audrey Hepburn : a biography / Martin Gitlin.
      p. cm. — (Greenwood biographies, ISSN 1540–4900)
  Includes bibliographical references and index.
  ISBN 978–0–313–35945–3 (alk. paper)
  1. Hepburn, Audrey, 1929–1993.   2. Motion picture actors and
actresses—United States—Biography.   I. Title.
  PN2287.H43G58 2009
  791.4302'8092—dc22
  [B]        2008042365

British Library Cataloguing in Publication Data is available.

Copyright © 2009 by Greenwood Publishing Group

All rights reserved. No portion of this book may be
reproduced, by any process or technique, without the
express written consent of the publisher.

Library of Congress Catalog Card Number: 2008042365
ISBN: 978–0–313–35945–3
ISSN: 1540–4900

First published in 2009

Greenwood Press, 88 Post Road West, Westport, CT 06881
An imprint of Greenwood Publishing Group, Inc.
www.greenwood.com

Printed in the United States of America

The paper used in this book complies with the
Permanent Paper Standard issued by the National
Information Standards Organization (Z39.48–1984).

10  9  8  7  6  5  4  3  2  1

*To my mother, Eleanor Gitlin, who has a gift for bringing a ray of sunshine to even my darkest days. Thanks, Mom.*

# CONTENTS

*Photo essay follows page 52*

# SERIES FOREWORD

In response to high school and public library needs, Greenwood developed this distinguished series of full-length biographies specifically for student use. Prepared by field experts and professionals, these engaging biographies are tailored for high school students who need challenging yet accessible biographies. Ideal for secondary school assignments, the length, format and subject areas are designed to meet educators' requirements and students' interests.

Greenwood offers an extensive selection of biographies spanning all curriculum-related subject areas including social studies, the sciences, literature and the arts, history and politics, as well as popular culture, covering public figures and famous personalities from all time periods and backgrounds, both historic and contemporary, who have made an impact on American and/or world culture. Greenwood biographies were chosen based on comprehensive feedback from librarians and educators. Consideration was given to both curriculum relevance and inherent interest. The result is an intriguing mix of the well known and the unexpected, the saints and sinners from long-ago history and contemporary pop culture. Readers will find a wide array of subject choices from fascinating crime figures like Al Capone to inspiring pioneers like Margaret Mead, from the greatest minds of our time like Stephen Hawking to the most amazing success stories of our day like J. K. Rowling.

While the emphasis is on fact, not glorification, the books are meant to be fun to read. Each volume provides in-depth information about the subject's life from birth through childhood, the teen years, and adulthood. A thorough account relates family background and education, traces personal and professional influences, and explores struggles, accomplishments, and contributions. A timeline highlights the most significant life events against a historical perspective. Bibliographies supplement the reference value of each volume.

# INTRODUCTION

Audrey Hepburn was beloved the world over and thought of by many as an angel. Despite coming of age in Nazi-occupied Holland and a somewhat rocky childhood, she managed to display a sense of goodness and humanity throughout many aspects of her life. The humility that defined Audrey appeared to be genuine. She shielded praise both professionally and personally not because modesty fit her image, but because it was part of her personality.

The last movie role for Audrey Hepburn was that of an angel. Many with a religious bent believed it to be good practice for her. Figuratively speaking, Audrey was viewed by many as an angel on earth, perhaps because she had witnessed firsthand man's brutality against his brother during World War II.

Audrey was shaped by her childhood experiences. The love for which she yearned throughout her life was a product of the abandonment by her father well before her teenage years. The insecurities that plagued her through most of her career were a result of the lack of praise she received from her mother as a youth. Her need to help those less fortunate came from watching her Dutch countrymen, many of them children, fall victim to the Nazis during the war. The pressure to excel that was both self-imposed and heaped on her by others during her adolescence shaped her desire for a simple, carefree life.

She didn't enter the entertainment world kicking and screaming, but she certainly required a firm push. Audrey was never one to embrace the flashing cameras and adulation of fans. While others in her position enjoyed the ego boost that would seem inherent in the ascension to stardom, she felt perplexed about and unworthy of the praise. Overwhelmed by the limelight, including the tremendous public and media scrutiny, and uncomfortable in the company of many in the haughty Hollywood crowd, Audrey continually sought to retreat to the loving arms of her family and the peaceful environment of a beautiful and sweet-smelling garden.

Audrey cared little that critics and fans believed she was doing her talent an injustice by using it so infrequently. While others of her era acted in a hundred or more movies, she played roles in just 25—and in none for seven years in the late 1960s and early 1970s. She spent the years that many actors consider to be their prime seeking inner peace and personal fulfillment.

Those who witnessed her magic on the silver screen offer that acting was Audrey's true calling. But she didn't find what she believed to be her true calling until she enticed smiles and brought hope to the children of the third world through her work with the United Nations Children's Fund (UNICEF) during the last years of her life. She didn't find her ideal love until those same years with Robert Wolders, whose love and respect for her was unmatched by any other man in her life and whom she considered too great a friend to marry.

But Audrey was the victim or (in her more contented moments) beneficiary of her own humility. The same lack of confidence that troubled her off camera permeated her performances on stage and screen. Audiences and critics embraced her weaknesses—they even identified with them. Ordinary moviegoers felt closer to her because of those imperfections, not despite them. Many of her finest characters—the princess in *Roman Holiday*, the Cockney flower girl in *My Fair Lady*, the terrorized blind woman in *Wait until Dark*—featured endearing vulnerabilities, but all had an inner strength that Audrey herself boasted. Though far from self-assured in her work, she always had the strength of her convictions, and so did the women she portrayed.

Audrey was always righteous in matters of the heart involving others, but never self-righteous. Though hurt time and again by the men in her life—at least until she met Robert—she never blamed them for the failures in their relationships, even the philandering of second husband Andrea Dotti. Instead, she gazed inward to examine what she could have done to save the marriage. In fact, many offered their amazement that she hadn't angrily terminated her marriage to Dotti.

Yet her righteousness seemed boundless in issues regarding the suffering of her fellow man, which came into play in her life the moment she stepped off a plane into a third world country whose people had fallen victim to starvation or drought or disease or war. She was uncompromising when speaking to world leaders as a representative of UNICEF about spending less money for the instruments of war and more money for the instruments of peace such as food and shelter and medicine and education. Her efforts, which tugged at the consciences of those world leaders, resulted in increased funding for those most in need. It sweetened the last year of her life when U.S. president George Bush utilized the military not to wage war, but to aid the hapless victims of war in Somalia. Audrey was more responsible than any celebrity for the greater focus and increased spending for humanitarian efforts regarding the needs of millions of people around the world.

That's what brought the greatest fulfillment to her life. Particular movie roles and the knowledge that she had performed well in them brought a certain amount of satisfaction. But there always seemed to be a hitch, whether it was a clash with a cast member, such as with Humphrey Bogart in *Sabrina,* or having her voice dubbed over by a professional singer in *My Fair Lady,* which ultimately cost her an Academy Award nomination.

Audrey never felt comfortable with the politics in the movie industry; rather, she felt a commitment to the people in her personal life. Early in her marriage to Mel Ferrer, she was accused of accepting roles only in movies in which he costarred or enjoyed a prominent role. Though that remains up to conjecture, she certainly awaited Mel to join her before taking her bows after theater productions. If she indeed wanted parts only in films with which Mel was involved, it was not a product of greed, but instead a need to remain close to the man she loved. And her habit of awaiting Mel to join her to soak in the applause of the audience was also a display of love and respect. The love and respect of those close to her, after all, always trumped professional success in the mind and heart of Audrey Hepburn.

Audrey was a woman with simple needs who enjoyed simple pleasures, yet she was caught up in a frenzied world of tremendous media scrutiny and public adulation. That is the primary reason she left the entertainment world from 1967 to 1975. She yearned to spend time with her family in her beloved Swiss home, where she could take walks, breathe the fresh air, and putter around in her garden.

But there was another factor in her retirement: Hollywood had changed. She had previously performed in an era in which films featured romance, in which sex was only implied and in which blood and gore rarely accompanied scenes of violence. By the middle to late 1960s, the sexual revolution had changed all artistic art forms. Sex and violence in the movies had become increasingly graphic, and Audrey wanted no part of it, though she did accept a few roles during a brief comeback.

Living within her emotional means motivated her early to escape. Audrey never dreamed about denying her desire for a simple life because it didn't clash with anything else. Fame meant nothing to her. Fortune proved only a means to take care of her family financially for generations to come. She even sent money to help the father who abandoned her and who showed little desire even to see her during her adult years. She could have lived in mansions and been waited on by servants who could tend to her every need, gardeners who could make beautiful flowers grow, and chefs who could spoil her with delicacies and desserts made with her favorite food, chocolate. But she lived in a modest home, tended to her own housework, spent time lovingly and passionately in her garden, and cooked her own meals.

And in the end, she preferred to fly coach to the most remote and depressing areas of the world to bring even an ounce of joy into the hopeless lives of people who had no idea who she was. There was no ego gratification to her work with UNICEF, but rather a feeling of goodness in her heart and soul.

It has been speculated that the illnesses rampant in the disease-ridden countries she visited played a role in her premature passing. If that is indeed the case, Audrey died as selflessly as she lived. And though she will always be remembered for her magical performances in the theater and on the silver screen, those she touched will cherish her more for her genuine humanitarianism.

# TIMELINE: EVENTS IN THE LIFE OF AUDREY HEPBURN

1929    Audrey Kathleen van Heemstra Ruston is born in Brussels, Belgium, on May 4.

1934    Audrey is sent to boarding school in Kent, England.

1935    The family is abandoned by father, Joseph.

1938    Audrey's parents officially divorce.

1939    Audrey moves with mother, Ella, and stepbrothers Ian and Alexander to Arnhem, Netherlands, where she studies ballet.

1940–1945    Audrey survives World War II in Nazi-occupied Holland, aiding the cause as part of the Dutch resistance.

1948    Audrey studies at the famed Marie Rambert ballet school and lands a bit part in the film *Dutch in Seven Lessons*.

1949    Audrey debuts in the London musical theater in both *High Button Shoes* and *Sauce Tartare*.

1950    Audrey lands a role in the London play *Sauce Piquante*.

1951    After playing bit parts on the British screen, Audrey receives her first big break, landing the lead role in a Broadway production of *Gigi*.

Engagement to James Hanson announced in the *London Times* on December 4.

1953    Audrey stars alongside Gregory Peck in her first Hollywood film, *Roman Holiday*.

1954    Audrey stars in a Broadway production of *Ondine*. She wins both an Oscar and a Golden Globe for her performance in

*Roman Holiday* as well as a Tony Award for her performance in *Ondine*.

Audrey marries American film actor Mel Ferrer in Switzerland on September 25.

1955   Audrey suffers her first miscarriage in the spring before shooting the epic film *War and Peace*.

1957   Audrey receives an opportunity to dance with Fred Astaire while starring in *Funny Face*.

1959   Audrey stars in *The Nun's Story*, *Green Mansions*, and her first western, *The Unforgiven*. While shooting the latter, she is thrown from a horse. Audrey has another miscarriage soon thereafter.

1960   Audrey gives birth to a son, Sean, on January 17.

1963   Audrey lands the role of Eliza Doolittle in the musical *My Fair Lady* but is dismayed to learn that her singing voice will be dubbed over.

1967   Audrey stars as a terrorized blind woman in *Wait until Dark*.

Mel and Audrey separate.

Audrey begins an eight-year hiatus from acting.

1968   Audrey meets Italian psychiatrist Dr. Andrea Dotti. The Ferrers divorce on December 5, as Audrey retains custody of Sean.

1969   Audrey marries Andrea Dotti on January 18.

1970   Audrey gives birth to a son, Luca, on February 8.

1976   Audrey returns to the screen in *Robin and Marian*.

1980   Audrey files for divorce from Dotti.

1981   Audrey meets Robert Wolders, who will remain her close companion for the rest of her life.

1982   Divorce from Dotti is finalized.

1984   Audrey's mother, Ella, dies on August 26.

1988   Audrey begins her work as a goodwill ambassador for the United Nations Children's Fund.

1992   Audrey is diagnosed with colon cancer and is informed by doctors that she has three months to live.

1993   Audrey passes away in her sleep on January 20, at 7:00 A.M., in her Switzerland home. Hundreds mourn at her funeral on January 24, while millions mourn worldwide.

# Chapter 1

# THE YOUNG ARISTOCRAT

If not for a forceful spanking, the world would never have known Audrey Hepburn. Even her family wouldn't have known her for more than six weeks.

Audrey Kathleen van Heemstra Ruston was born in Brussels, Belgium, on May 4, 1929. Three weeks later, she contracted a near-deadly case of whooping cough. Her mother, Ella, a strict Christian Scientist, refused to have her diagnosed by a doctor, opting instead to pray for her daughter's recovery. But those prayers were not immediately answered. Eventually, after one particularly severe coughing attack, Audrey's heart stopped, and she began turning blue. Her hysterical nanny summoned Ella, who revived her daughter by praying fervently while swatting her behind. Audrey's son Sean has speculated that the awareness of a second chance at life motivated her through all her years.

This iconic figure, revered as an actor, was also known for her petite figure. But Audrey was a roly-poly infant with chubby cheeks and a round belly. Her prodigious appetite only served to add to her girth. Audrey rather humorously stated that she drank more milk than did her two half brothers combined. The baby fat quickly disappeared, revealing Audrey as a stunningly pretty child. But the beauty on the outside was contrasted by turmoil on the inside, caused in part by a dysfunctional family life.

Audrey's mother, Baroness Ella van Heemstra, rarely missed an opportunity to remind anyone, least of all her husband, Joseph Victor Anthony Hepburn-Ruston, of the long line of Dutch nobility in her ancestry. Ella was brought up in extreme wealth. Her parents owned a country mansion, a city house, and a summer cottage. She spent most of her youth in the

Hague, the Dutch capital, but spent vacations, weekends, and summers flitting about the family's ancestral home at Doorn. She was surrounded by creature comforts and beauty, particularly at the estate, which featured a castle and moat as well as thousands of beautiful tulips, which she often counted as she whiled away the hours. She certainly spent little time on chores—Ella was doted on by servants catering to her every whim.

Indeed, Ella had everything she wanted in life but one thing: she desperately wished to pursue acting, but her father forbade it. He considered the profession to be beneath the dignity not only of his daughter, but also of his family's ancestral heritage. She dutifully obeyed her father, but Audrey later confessed her feeling that Ella never recovered emotionally from the disappointment over being disallowed to fulfill her aspirations. Some believe she pushed Audrey into a show business career, an opinion that seems more justified when considering Ella's own shattered professional dreams.

Like the vast majority of women of earlier generations, Ella was strongly encouraged to consider her future only in terms of finding the ideal gentleman to wed. And in the world of aristocracy in which Ella was raised, only a man brought up in the same station in life would suffice. That man proved to be the Honorable Jan Hendrik Gustaaf Adolf Quarles van Ufford, whom she married three months before her 20th birthday. That man proved to be no fit for Ella. The couple argued incessantly. As was the case with many men in that era, particularly those of wealth and breeding, he had been raised to believe that the husband was the unquestioned master of any marital relationship. But Ella refused to accede to his demands for her subservience. The result was that she attempted to break away on three occasions, only to be persuaded by her father to return to the marriage and patch up their differences for the benefit of sons Alexander and Ian. But after five years of wedded misery, such considerations were no longer enough for Ella to remain attached to a man she had grown to despise. The couple was divorced in 1925.

Divorce was quite uncommon among aristocratic couples of that generation, but Ella preferred that option to infidelity. She had a weakness for attractive men, which also played a role in her yearning to leave her husband. Shortly after the divorce, she accompanied her sons to Paramibo, the capital of the South American country of Suriname, a Dutch territory of which her father had been appointed governor in 1921. Ella, a social butterfly who enjoyed all the trappings of wealth and privilege, didn't consider living in that remote, primitive nation suitable to her lifestyle, despite the fact that she enjoyed all the benefits that being the daughter of a high-ranking official had to offer. A year after arriving in Suriname, she took Alexander and Ian back briefly to the Dutch town of Arnhem, then to Indonesia. Her purpose in settling there was to reestablish a relationship with Joseph Hepburn-Ruston, whom she had met three years earlier as her marriage began failing. The spark between the two remained strong. Hepburn-Ruston was a 37-year-old Anglo-Irish businessman who had joined the diplomatic service after World War I and was placed in the Dutch East Indies before leaving that post to work for Maclaine Watson and Company, which dealt in the East Indian tin trade.

There were two problems, however. First, Joseph was still married. Second, he was living off the inheritance of his wife, Cornelia. But he was quite attracted to Ella and her title. He often introduced her as a baroness even though after her divorce, Ella was forced to accept an office job to support her boys. Various historical descriptions of Joseph range from dashing and professionally ambitious to ordinary and lazy. But by all accounts, he saw the possibility of marrying Ella as an opportunity to work his way into a family in which he could relax and enjoy the benefits of wealth. Ella, on the other hand, sought a father for her two sons. Joseph's charm and generosity disarmed Ella, who was easily flattered. He pampered her and showered her with attention, which further showed his devotion. His indulgence all but assured their future together. Only a year after Ella divorced her first husband, she married Hepburn-Ruston.

Neither, however, embraced living in the East Indies. Its oppressive heat and lack of social attractions motivated the couple to return to Europe. Joseph finagled a transfer to London, but he had always been rather restless. A year later, Maclaine Watson and Company fit him with the title of vice president and deputy administrator and instructed him to open a branch office in Belgium. The couple soon settled in Brussels, where it became apparent immediately that Joseph indeed wanted to spoil his wife, but with her own money. He became disillusioned when he discovered, to his dismay, that the van Heemstra family wasn't as prosperous as he had believed. Along with Ella's disenchantment with life in Brussels, which she considered rather staid, their marriage became difficult.

Into this setting, Audrey was born. She was a shy child, one who displayed a natural, reserved air and charm that played a role in making her so attractive on the movie screen. She didn't play with dolls, as many girls did; rather, she preferred the company of animals such as birds, puppies, and kittens. She boasted a vivid imagination from the beginning, creating in her mind a fairy castle from the most easily identifiable of nature's wonders such as a tree or bush. Audrey's imaginative side was also nourished through reading, particularly the works of authors such as Rudyard Kipling, a writer of children's literature whose talents were appreciated by her brother Alexander and passed on to her. She thoroughly enjoyed Kipling's adventurous tales but admitted that one reason she devoured his works was because Alexander did as well, and she wanted to be just like her brother. As she approached her teenage years, her literary interests veered in another direction. She began soaking in suspenseful works about romance and intrigue by authors such as Edgar Wallace and Edward Phillips Oppenheim, rather than the sweet, rather mundane books preferred by her peers. She did, however, enjoy classics that have been cherished by schoolgirls for generations such as *The Secret Garden* and *Heidi*.

Then there was music, which sent little Audrey into fits of rapture. The phonograph turning 78 rpm classical records often entertained the Hepburn family, but Audrey most of all. She was swept away by the sweet strains of symphonies from such composers as Bach and Beethoven. Audrey and her mother, with whom she developed an immediate emotional attachment, attended concerts by the renowned Concertgebouw Orchestra of the Hague, which appeared seasonally in Brussels. Like many little girls of her generation, Audrey also enjoyed the ballet. As she watched the dancers perform, she dreamed of being on that very stage. But watching the lithe ballet dancers also brought out dissatisfaction with her appearance. Like many girls careening toward their teenage years, she became obsessed with the smallest imperfections and avoided even the slightest glance in the mirror. She considered her eyes to be bulging and her teeth crooked. She had also not begun to resemble the actor who would never exceed 103 pounds, aside from during her pregnancies, throughout her professional career. Audrey couldn't seem to work off all her baby fat, even through tomboyish activities such as tree climbing and running around the neighborhood with her brothers. She despised her chubby elbows and dimpled knees and was depressed when she compared herself physically to the petite ballet dancers for whom she felt great admiration. Yet her sweet tooth continued to get the best of her. Audrey adored cookies and chocolate. Even the smallest of treats seemed to take a toll on her body as a child.

Though Audrey and her mother grew close through their shared appreciation of the arts, several other aspects of their relationship proved difficult. The baroness seemed unhappy most of the time. Audrey attributed that fact at least partly to her mother's own weight problems; she was constantly attempting to lose about 25 pounds. Along with suspicions of her husband's desire to meet other women, Ella simply couldn't find peace of mind. She became critical and intolerant of her children, on whom she sometimes took out her frustrations. Though Audrey was appreciative of her mother's efforts, the nurturing and tender loving care all children need were things she had to look elsewhere to find.

"My mother was not a very affectionate person," Audrey said. "She was a fabulous mother, but she had a Victorian upbringing of great discipline, of great ethics. She was very strict, very demanding of her children. She had a lot of love within her, but she was not always able to show it. I went searching all over the place to find somebody who would cuddle me, and I found it, in my aunts and nannies."[1]

Fortunately, there was never any shortage of nannies in the home. Unfortunately, they couldn't sequester Audrey away from the constant bickering between her parents. Joseph and Ella argued incessantly. Audrey understood instinctively that her parents were suffering from an unhealthy marriage, but she was simply too young to help soothe the tensions. Instead, Audrey became more introspective and emotionally delicate. She would hide from her parents, taking solace only when her father was away on one of his many business trips.

Ella became somewhat alarmed at Audrey's sensitivity and shyness, so she took a bold step in an attempt to force her five-year-old daughter to open up by sending her to a boarding school in England. Audrey was horribly frightened at being away from her mother at such a young age. Her classmates tormented her about her chubbiness and lack of confidence as well as her struggles with the English language. But in her adult years, she admitted that the experience gave her at least a small sense of independence that proved beneficial. And her schooling wasn't her only taste of England. To further her daughter's education in life, Ella had Audrey spend holidays with a coal miner's family in the English countryside.

But though little Audrey had become accustomed to her routine in England, other events in that European country produced a storm not only over its political scene, but on her parents as well. By the mid-1930s, the burgeoning Fascist movement begun by Italian dictator Benito Mussolini and strengthened brutally by German Nazi leader Adolf Hitler had taken hold in other European countries. The fever was catching, even in a nation steeped in freedom and democracy such as England, where Sir Oswald Mosley formed the British Union of Fascists (BUF). Among Mosley's sympathizers was future wife Diana Mitford, who had been friends with Ella. Audrey's mother soon encouraged her passionately anti-Communist husband to join. Ella and Joseph became so involved in fundraising and recruitment for Oswald that the former felt compelled to write a glowing endorsement of him for the BUF weekly newspaper in 1935. The letter praised Oswald greatly.

Soon thereafter, Audrey's parents accompanied Mosley and a British Fascist delegation to Germany to see the Nazis in action firsthand. They not only toured the country to witness the changes that had been made, but they posed for a photo with Hitler at his Brown House headquarters in Munich. Ella eventually framed it and placed it proudly on the mantelpiece in the Hepburn-Ruston home.

It has been speculated that Ella's involvement with the Fascist movement was more a means to promote togetherness with Joseph than a genuine belief in its principles and ideals. It has also been theorized that she hoped to support her husband and his dreams of ascending in Oswald's organization. It didn't matter which was the case in the end, however, because Ella's plans ultimately backfired. Joseph became so involved in the Fascist movement that he left Ella as soon as they returned from Germany in May 1935, leaving behind Audrey and her two half brothers in the process. Though some believe that the strain between Ella and Joseph over his alleged alcoholism played the most prominent role in his departure, most of those close to the family have offered that he was motivated by his increased political passions. In fact, he soon broke away from the BUF to hook up with a more violently anti-Semitic group. Ella's father accused him not just of mismanaging the family assets, but also of funneling some of the money into Fascist interests.

The reasons behind her parents' sudden split didn't matter to little Audrey. All she knew was that her father was gone. She described the event as the most traumatic in her life, one from which she admitted that she never fully recovered. Audrey knew nothing about politics. She did know that she loved and looked up to her father and simply needed him in her life. She grew jealous of her friends, all of whom still had fathers in their households. And she could hardly bear to watch the effect the breakup had on her mother. She recalled 50 years later,

> I was destroyed at the time and cried for days and days. My parents' divorce was the first big blow I had as a child....I worshipped my father and missed him terribly from the day he disappeared. Having my father cut off from me when I was only six was desperately awful. If I could just have seen him regularly, I would have felt he loved me. But as it was, I always envied other people's fathers, came home with tears because they had a daddy. My mother had great love for me, but she was not always able to show it. I had no one to cuddle me.[2]

The loss of her father as a consistent figure in Audrey's life brought the addition of her maternal grandparents. They gathered up Audrey and Ella and took them to the family home in Arnhem, which rests about 50 miles southeast of Amsterdam. Meanwhile, Joseph relocated to London and asked for visitation rights. To everyone's surprise, Ella granted that request. She believed that Audrey would benefit from having a father in her life, but she overestimated Joseph. He brought Audrey back to London on occasion, but those visits were soon curtailed. She ended up seeing her father about once a year during the period in which she attended a small private girls' school in Kent. Though Joseph sometimes visited Kent, on most occasions, he avoided Audrey. Instead, he frequented the town to work with British Nazi propagandist Arthur Tester. On the other hand, Ella had disassociated herself from Mosley and the BUF by 1937. She had been taken aback by news of Nazi brutality in Germany and came to regret her work with Mosley and the excursion to meet Hitler.

In the meantime, Audrey was trying unsuccessfully to adjust to home life without her father. Her love of chocolate went from a simple pleasure to an obsession. And while most girls her age were busy playing with dolls, Audrey couldn't even stomach the thought. It reminded her too much of her own unhappy family situation. She said,

> I never played with dolls. Mother would often lament this fact, since I was her only daughter and she liked the idea of my dressing up the things and combing their awful blond hair. But the real reason I didn't like them is that I felt I had to play house with them, and I didn't want to bring up all the pain of what my own home life was like. We went from loud screaming matches that were never resolved, to utter silence, like a cloistered existence. It was extremely perplexing. It hurt too much. I didn't want to talk about it. I preferred to ignore it.[3]

Though she became distant from her friends and unhappy at school, greatly because of the separation of her parents, the time spent in London before World War II brought her a world of entertainment that would play a critical role in developing her professional ambitions. She and Ella soaked in fine musical theater and plays written by such legends as Somerset Maugham and Noel Coward. Audrey became fascinated by a genre of British entertainment comedy known as the Christmas pantomime, in which men dressed as women and women dressed as men. She was enraptured by the lavish productions and enchanted by the fairy-tale stories that made the shows suitable for kids. Audrey also fell in love with the children's classic *Peter Pan*.

Despite her dissatisfaction with her body, or perhaps because of it, Audrey began taking weekly ballet lessons at the age of nine. Her fierce dedication to the art dwarfed that of her fellow students. Though rather uncoordinated, her discipline and passion allowed her to master a variety of steps. She fell in love with dancing. On one occasion, her mother showed up just in time to watch Audrey featured in a recital. It was Audrey's 10th birthday, on May 4, 1939, and she danced proudly for her mother. Audrey was ecstatic as her mother joined her classmates and teacher in enthusiastic applause. But early that September, a year after her divorce had been finalized, Ella paid another visit to the dance studio. Audrey's dance instructor had hoped to continue working with her pupil, whom she believed showed tremendous potential. When asked by the instructor if she could take Audrey back to London to continue her lessons, Ella replied that her daughter would be accompanying her back to Belgium.

England had just declared war on Germany. The Nazis had invaded Poland just days earlier. Ella believed the family would be much safer in Holland, which had yet been drawn into the war. But soon, no country in Europe would be safe from German attack. Ella understood the potential dangers of being separated from Audrey during a war. In hindsight, it might have appeared foolish to move Audrey from England to Holland. Both eventually felt Nazi brutality from the skies, but the preparation for war allowed England to move its children to the safer countryside, while Holland was invaded and bombed unmercifully for its refusal to submit to German terror. At the time, however, all Ella knew was that Holland had declared its neutrality and that England had declared war.

It wasn't easy getting Audrey back to Holland. Plane reservations were at a premium, so soon after the start of hostilities, despite the fact that England and France did virtually nothing to help the Poles and didn't begin fighting in earnest until the latter was invaded in May 1940, the family managed to secure one of the last planes traveling from England to Holland. It marked the last time Audrey would ever see her father, whose conversion to Nazism was complete. He had gone from helping finance Nazi propaganda to marching in parades with the Fascist Black Shirts and being pelted with rocks by angry protesters. Eventual British prime minister Winston Churchill claimed that if he ever gained power in England, Mosley and his cohorts would be shipped off to jail for the rest of the war. Indeed, Joseph was among hundreds of English Fascists sent to the Isle of Man on house arrest, though it has never been proven that he helped the Nazi cause in any way during wartime. Meanwhile, though Audrey inherently understood that Nazism was evil despite her lack of political awareness, she still hoped in vain that her parents would reunite.

Despite Arnhem's proximity to the German border, Audrey couldn't have felt any further from danger. The mostly wealthy citizens of the beautiful, quaint Dutch town lived peacefully as Poland was being destroyed.

Ella, Audrey, and the van Heemstras celebrated a festive Christmas in 1939 with Ian, Alexander, and a host of relatives. Audrey enjoyed the company of one and all. The joys of the holiday season helped Audrey at least temporarily forget the misery she still felt over the demise of her parents' marriage.

It was the period of the so-called phony war. The German blitzkrieg had demolished Poland, but neither England nor France was confronting the Nazis. The Dutch seemed safe. Audrey enrolled at the Arnhem Conservatory of Music and Dance. Though still a bit awkward, her skills began to improve. Though the school was not among the most distinguished in Europe, the instructors did help Audrey with her posture and flexibility. Adorned with the best ballet shoes, leotards, and tutus Ella could afford, Audrey developed a strong sense of pride in her performance. She took her ballet lessons quite seriously, displaying a determination that would prove valuable in her future professional life. She rarely joined in on the giggling and other mindless fun enjoyed by her fellow students, who were simply participating in dance because they loved it. Audrey was obsessed with ballet dancing because she considered it her future. Excelling had become her life's mission. She began reading about the careers of such ballet stars as Vaslav Nijinsky and Anna Pavlova, the Russian dancer who had become her idol. While other young girls fantasized about becoming movie stars, Audrey had no knowledge about any stars of the silver screen, greatly due to Ella's lack of interest in film.

Ella, who was quite involved with the local arts council, did encourage her daughter's involvement in the arts. On one occasion, Ella gave a reading of a poem titled "Daughter" to an audience at the Arnhem Theater, to which Audrey listened joyfully from the balcony. Ella and her family also joined together in late 1939 to perform a musical tribute to Mozart at that same location.

Perilously close to the German border, Arnhem was prepared for war by the spring of 1940. Barbed wire fences had been constructed near the van Heemstra estate. Dutch soldiers anxiously walked through the streets of the town or were being transported through Arnhem in preparation for combat. Audrey was understandably frightened, as she could hear periodic bursts of gunfire coming from near the border. Though the Germans had yet to begin their invasion, skirmishes signaled that hostilities were close at hand.

Audrey, meanwhile, continued to be withdrawn. The Arnhem Day School balked at enrolling her due to her weak command of the Dutch language after she had spent so much of her academic life in England. She was embarrassed to raise her hand and speak in class due to her fear of being ridiculed and laughed at by her fellow students. But when she studied ballet, all her insecurities and fears melted away. And when she heard that the renowned Sadler's Wells Ballet would be visiting Holland in May 1940, Audrey was thrilled. It was, after all, considered the premier ballet company in England and among the finest in Europe. The tour through countries being threatened by Germany, such as France, Holland, and Belgium, was considered quite courageous. Audrey counted the days until she could see the immensely talented dancers, led by Margot Fonteyn, and also featuring Robert Helpmann, arguably the most brilliant mime of his generation. During their Dutch visit, the troupe was based in the Hague, from which they traveled to various locations.

The troupe members feared that all hell was about to break loose. And they were right.

## NOTES

1. Barry Paris, *Audrey Hepburn* (New York: G. P. Putnam's Sons, 1996), 7–8.

2. Alexander Walker, *Audrey: Her Real Story* (New York: St. Martin's Griffin, 1994), 14–15.

3. Diana Maychick, *Audrey Hepburn: An Intimate Portrait* (New York: Carol, 1993), 19.

# Chapter 2

# WAR CHILD

The Sadler's Wells Ballet performed in Arnhem on May 9, 1940, four days after Audrey's 11th birthday. Audrey eagerly awaited that evening, during which she wore a long dress for the first time in her life. Ella had arranged to give a speech of thanks to the company both in Dutch and in English, after which her daughter was to present a bouquet of tulips and roses at the end of the night to legendary Sadler's Wells Ballet director Ninette de Valois. But there was a method to what the troupe considered to be Ella's madness in elongating the festivities with the Nazis poised on the border. Ella hoped to convince the Nazi collaborators she suspected to be in the audience that she was a pro-Nazi aristocrat and was holding up the proceedings to allow the German invaders to push through against little resistance. She hoped to use her cover to continue her clandestine activities against the Nazis. The company nervously accepted the kind words and flowers before hightailing it out of Arnhem in the nick of time.

As tensions mounted in Europe, Ella had become quite involved in helping create a Dutch resistance movement in the likely scenario of a German takeover. The movement revolved around activities in Arnhem, where Ella hosted informal gatherings in an attempt to add more volunteers to the resistance. Royalty, aristocrats, and commoners all offered ideas to be included in a grand plan. Ella, who had been criticized by many for what they perceived to be snobbery, began to embrace the notion that courage, a strong will, and creative thought were more meaningful than class distinction. An air of intrigue gripped the community. Everyone particularly committed to the resistance had to be wary of his or her neighbor, for one never knew who could be a Nazi sympathizer. After all, Nazi spies were busily circulating around the area, so rather than having typical conversations, people spoke in codes. Every word, every action took on heightened importance. Audrey said,

> I don't remember what all the things stood for, but I do know that if someone mentioned rijstaffel [the Dutch national dish of fish, meat, vegetable, and subtle spices], that meant there were lots of ears around and listening! You were supposed to be careful of what you were saying.... We all had to be very secretive until it was clear whose side our neighbors were on. And since the Dutch are known to be rather close to the vest anyway, we often were surprised when we discovered other resisters. Some of the most laconic people worked the hardest for the cause.[1]

Their efforts were eventually rewarded, but not before a period of hardship and agony the extent of which the Dutch people had never previously experienced. Though accounts vary on the initial force of the attack on their little helpless nation, what is certain is that a period of darkness and despair soon fell on the people of Arnhem and their neighbors. Just minutes after the Sadler's Wells Ballet company departed, the Nazis arrived. According to various reports, German parachutists filled the sky; sirens, air-raid alarms, and gunshots and artillery could be heard throughout the area; and bitter street fighting motivated frightened residents to hide in their homes. But Audrey told quite a different story. "All civilians were ordered to remain indoors and to close their shutters, and we were warned not to look out the windows," Audrey recalled. "Naturally, we all peeped.... It was uncannily strange. In an invasion, one expects fighting; but there was no fighting. We saw the gray uniforms of the German soldiers on foot. They all held machine guns and marched in looking spick-and-span and disciplined; then came the rumble of the trucks—and the next thing we knew was that they had taken complete charge of the town."[2]

The Germans displayed far more brutality in major cities such as Rotterdam, Amsterdam, and the Hague, all of which they bombed unmercifully with no declaration of war. The firebombing of Rotterdam was especially catastrophic, as 30,000 civilians were killed and 11,000 buildings destroyed. Help came neither from the British nor the French, who were now bracing for the attacks on their own countries. Dutch commander in chief General H. G. Winkelman planned to surrender the northern and eastern areas of the country and await reinforcements from the British.

But England was busy with political matters, replacing prime minister and Hitler appeaser Neville Chamberlain with Winston Churchill. The tiny Dutch army fought with bravery, inflicting some damage to the German invaders, but was soon overwhelmed. Nazi paratroopers dropped into the Hague to capture Queen Wilhelmina, who was spirited away to England for safety.

Strangely, however, the night of the ballet and German attack became etched in Audrey's mind as the point at which she found her calling. Despite her fears, she felt alive in the belief that a career beckoned:

> It was for me a most amazing night. I was too exhilarated about meeting Fonteyn to be as frightened as I should have been about the war. It was almost as if the bombing started and the shooting became constant because I had screwed up my courage and told my idol that I wanted to be a dancer just like she was! The sounds were like fireworks to me, an affirmation that I had desires and I finally voiced them. Oddly enough, I think my depression began to lift that night. It wasn't until morning that I realized it was damp in the basement, that there were mice and even rats, and I was shivering. All these things were true, and I began to feel them, and the fear of death, but everything was also finally all right. I had discovered a purpose in my life. I was to become a dancer.[3]

As an 11-year-old child, Audrey simply didn't comprehend the depth of despair she and her fellow countrymen were about to experience. Five days after the invasion, with Rotterdam a pile of rubble and Queen Wilhelmina in exile, Winkelman's troops surrendered. Ella and the Dutch resistance had done their part, joining forces to blow up trains, bridges, and ammunition dumps to hinder the invaders. Some members of the resistance were caught and executed as a lesson to anyone who dared to commit anti-Nazi acts. One was Ella's brother Willem, an attorney whom Ella had persuaded to join the resistance. He was killed by firing squad in the town square along with five others after bravely blowing up a train filled with German soldiers. Audrey and her devastated mother shed many a tear over his death. They became further distraught by the loss of Ella's nephew Frans, who was executed by the Germans for his resistance activities. Ella began to question her own motives in the movement but continued to hold secret meetings in her basement.

Meanwhile, the German blitzkrieg that had overrun Poland was simply too powerful. In the following weeks, the good citizens of Arnhem were reminded every day that their country had been incorporated into the Third Reich. The city's newspapers and radio station had come under government control.

The Germans, who criminally squeezed every bit of wealth from the aristocratic families in each country in their growing sphere, quickly dev-astated the Van Heemstras financially. Though the family was allowed to remain in its ancestral home, the invaders confiscated all their gold, and their silver money was replaced by zinc. Their bank accounts and securities were liquidated and their personal jewelry was looted. The van Heemstras went from rich to poor in short order.

Ella also feared for her daughter's safety because of her English-sounding name and background as well as the fact that she spoke that language. Au-drey was therefore enrolled in school as Edda van Heemstra, rather than Audrey Kathleen Ruston, and instructed to speak Dutch. She maintained her new identity for the duration of the war. Her schooling changed dra-matically as the Germans Nazified the faculty and the curriculum. The League of Netherlands Teachers was forced to give its allegiance to the Third Reich and instruct the students not only how to speak German, but in the falsified history that blamed the hapless Jews for virtually every evil in human existence. In addition, the Germans displayed a lack of interest in the conditions at Dutch schools. Audrey's classroom remained unheated through the winter months.

Life soon returned to as normal as one could expect under the cir-cumstances, though rationing kept the German occupiers well fed and clothed and the Dutch scrambling to make ends meet. All mail, rail, and telephone services were back within a month, however, as were sports activities such as swimming and soccer. The population used movies as a diversion, but the entertaining films from Britain and America had been replaced by those from Germany, which were filled with propaganda about its triumphant army and the glories of the Third Reich.

Fortunately for Audrey, the least political of all school subjects was music. Though the works of all Jewish composers were *verboten* in German-occupied territories, the symphonies of Austrians and Ger-mans, such as Bach, Beethoven, and Mozart, were still enjoyed. And so was ballet, which not only continued to motivate Audrey, but which she used to aid the Dutch resistance. Some of the money she earned teach-ing dancing and piano to younger girls at the conservatory was given to the underground, for which she claimed to have worked constantly, despite the grave danger. She knew that 70 Dutch children had been sent to prison for planning to destroy Nazi cables and gas supply centers, but her hatred for the Nazis and everything they represented motivated her to take the risk. Dutch author L. De Jong expressed the spirit of the resistance:

> As general obstructionism, both passive and active, grew throughout the entire country, youth followed the example of their elders. The adolescents were fully aware of what had happened to their Fatherland; the younger and youngest sensed the true and tragic state of affairs.... They were told that the Queen and the princely family had been forced to leave the Netherlands and were staying in foreign countries. They wondered at the strange men in outlandish uniforms, speaking an incomprehensible language. And with all the spontaneity of a child's mind that does not think of ultimate results, that lives for the moment only, these youthful patriots threw themselves into the battle against the occupying power and against the traitors.[4]

Two of those youthful patriots were Audrey's half brothers, Alexander and Ian, who refused to join the Netherland Institute of Folkish Education, a Nazification youth group located near Arnhem in which boys fitting the Aryan ideal underwent arduous physical training before joining the Nazi movement. Alexander's recalcitrance landed him in a forced labor camp in Germany for the rest of the war. Ian was deemed too young to work and was left behind, but Audrey was distraught over the departure of her older half brother and pined for him in vain to return. She and her family would secretly listen to Freedom Radio for any Allied successes in the European theater of the war, but good news would not be forthcoming until at least 1943.

The nightmarish terror that had spread throughout Europe, particularly after Germany invaded the Soviet Union in June 1941, was being felt in Arnhem. In the same month of Germany's attack on the Soviet Union, about 700 young Jewish Dutch men were sent to Buchenwald, a concentration camp in Germany, where they were murdered. Their parents were informed that their ashes would be returned to their families for the right price. Arthur Seyss-Inquart, the traitor who turned Austria over to the Nazis and had been named Reichskommissar of the Netherlands, declared that the Jews had no place among the Dutch people.

Non-Jews didn't escape the brutality. In one day in May 1942, 70 Dutch were executed as a reprisal for alleged crimes against the occupiers, while hundreds of others were slaughtered for coming to the aid of British pilots who had been shot down over their Dutch homeland. Audrey was a witness to the atrocities and brutality Germany inflicted on the occupied peoples, including the Jews, who were being rounded up and herded away into cattle cars for deportation to Germany and Poland, for their eventual extermination. "Families with babies, little children being hauled into meat wagons, wooden vans with just a slat at the top, and all those faces starting out at you," visualized Audrey. "I knew the cold clutch of human terror all through my early teens; I saw it, felt it, heard it—and it never goes away. You see, it wasn't just a nightmare; I was there, and it all happened."[5]

Audrey received her first lessons in acting when she pretended to be uncaring about such tragedies for her role in the resistance. It mattered not that the German occupiers had stolen nearly everything her family owned and that she and Ian barely had enough food on which to subsist. She pretended to be oblivious to the tragedies and danger surrounding her as she strolled happily along the streets of Arnhem to deliver secret coded messages to the underground that she had hidden in her shoe. Audrey would even peel off from the school playground to share food with downed Allied pilots in the woods. On one occasion in 1942, Ella sent her to find a British paratrooper in a nearby forest and invite him to stay at their home overnight. But after she made contact with him, she noticed a German soldier approaching. Thinking quickly, Audrey stooped down and grabbed a bunch of daisies and began pulling the petals out one by one. She smiled nicely at the German soldier, who believed her to be simply playing in the forest, then offered him the bouquet. He grabbed it, patted Audrey on the head, and walked off unaware that the little girl had just made arrangements to give comfort to the enemy.

Audrey received her comfort from dancing. She displayed enough talent and potential to study under Winja Marova at the Arnhem School of Music. Marova had touted herself as a former Russian ballerina, but she was actually Dutch, her real name was Winnie Koopman, and she was married to Douwe Draaisma, the director of the school. Nevertheless, that Marova accepted Audrey as a student was considered quite a feat and opportunity. And Audrey responded by becoming one of her premier dancers. Marova later expressed wonderment at her student's work ethic and talent as well as her natural ability to turn on charm and engage an audience. The young teen's success cemented her desire to become a ballerina. And Ella supported that dream, spending a great deal of time with her daughter at rehearsals and behind the curtains during performances. Though Ella has been accused of being a stage mother, there is no evidence she at any time pursued the spotlight for herself. Her own dreams of being a performer had been shattered years earlier, and Ella showed no desire to recapture them.

Ella had other priorities at that time, such as keeping herself and her family alive. The Germans tightened the noose around the Netherlands in 1943 as the threat of an Allied invasion of Europe grew. Partaking in resistance activities had become increasingly dangerous, but the crimes of the German occupiers had also become increasingly obvious. Unlike many Austrians, the Dutch never embraced Nazism. One in 10 Jews in the Netherlands were at one point or another hidden or given a new identity by brave Dutchmen during the war, including the unforgettable Anne Frank. And only a sprinkling of college students joined the Dutch Nazi Party.

Though just a young teenager and limited by her youth, Audrey continued to play a role in the resistance. She forged signatures on identity cards and would carry messages to members of the Dutch underground. She grew more excited about the intrigue than frightened by the potential dangers of her missions. During her later years, she would recall all the whispering, hand gestures, and facial signals, all of which took on different meanings and were indelibly etched in her brain.

The thrill of participating in the resistance was tempered by a rather morose home life. Ella had fallen into a severe depression since her eldest son had been shipped off to the labor camp in Germany. The family had not heard one word about his fate. Audrey and Ian received little attention from their mother, whose energies were being drained by the grieving over her missing son and by her own resistance activities. The lack of food had reached crisis proportions. Young Ian would sometimes hold his stomach and cry for nourishment.

But Audrey, who was able to relieve some of the hardship by giving dancing lessons, didn't feel the pangs of hunger at the time. She had been subsisting on lettuce, unappetizing bread made with peas, and an occasional potato. When the potatoes ran out, she would eat tulip bulbs. Audrey soon slipped to ninety pounds and lost energy, but she continued to teach dance to help the underground and her family. It mattered not if her students were children of the resistance or Nazi sympathizers, as long as they were willing to pay her for her services. Audrey was emaciated, but then, so it seemed, were all the Dutch children. Only the German occupiers were keeping their bellies full.

During one teaching session, a starving Audrey leaned over, felt the blood rushing to her brain, then blacked out. After she was revived, a janitor chastised her for her lack of eating and brought her with him to a large closet, from which he hauled down a huge ball of Edam cheese. The janitor had been saving the cheese for just the right charitable case and deemed Audrey to be the ideal candidate. A small piece of the cheese perked her up, but it also caused a stomach ailment since Audrey had gone so long without nourishment. She took pride in the fact that by using mind over matter, she sustained herself for quite a while without a steady intake of food.

Audrey continued to combine her love of dance with her work for the resistance. She and fellow dancers would put on performances at the homes of brave underground workers, including the van Heemstra residence on several occasions. They would lock the doors and windows, draw the blinds, dim the lights, and perform routines that Audrey had choreographed herself, as her friend played the piano and a lookout scanned the area for German soldiers. And because of the fear of retribution, not a soul would clap when the show ended. The last order of business was passing a hat, into which those who could afford it would place money to buoy the resistance movement.

Eventually, the recitals stopped. Audrey had been so weakened by a lack of food that she could no longer dance, but she and thousands of others continued to be small cogs in the giant machinery of resistance. Among those she most admired was a secret society of university students called the "Beggars" who killed Nazi soldiers one by one and dumped them into nearby canals. Many of those brave students were discovered and executed by the Nazis. Among those who couldn't escape Nazi terror was Ian. It is unknown whether he was among the group of university students, but he was taken to Berlin to work at a munitions factory. His fate was a mystery to Ella and Audrey until the war ended.

Following the war, Audrey read *The Diary of Anne Frank* and found an amazing parallel between her experiences and those of the doomed girl, who was discovered in Amsterdam in 1944 and murdered at the Auschwitz concentration camp. Frank was forced into hiding and, as a Jewish girl, lived a far more perilous existence, but from devouring the book that she would eventually memorize, Audrey understood all the emotions and feelings that poured from the author's heart and mind. She marveled at the optimism and faith in human nature expressed by the imprisoned girl with whom she had so much in common.

"It was a different corner of Holland, [but] all the events I experienced were so incredibly accurately described by her—not just what was going on on the outside, but was going on on the inside of a young girl starting to be a woman…all in a cage," Audrey said. "She expresses the claustrophobia, but transcends it through her love of nature, her awareness of humanity and her love—real love—of life."[6]

Audrey, meanwhile, was displaying a real love of ballet. She continued to be Morova's prize pupil into January 1944, when she performed

in a student showcase that her teacher had choreographed at the Arnhem City Theater. Billed as Audrey Hepburn-Ruston, she was featured
in several numbers and was noted to have performed brilliantly. But it
was at that point that she had become so frail and weak that Marova told
Ella that Audrey should stop dancing temporarily. By that time, the van
Heemstra family was subsisting on barely edible bread made with peas and
a watery soup. Many of their countrymen were trying to cook grass, but
Audrey simply couldn't stomach that.

She also couldn't stomach that the Germans removed all radios from
Dutch homes, which they did in 1943 as a means of keeping the people
in the dark about the war. But news trickled in during the summer of
1944 about the Allied invasion of Europe and the liberation of Paris, as
the retreating Germans began to populate the area. In fact, about 80,000
Germans who had lost the arrogance they had as conquerors shuffled their
way into Holland. But the war was far from over. An historic battle was
about to unfold in the heart of Arnhem.

British general Bernard Montgomery had drawn up a plan called "Operation Market Garden," in which Allied airborne and ground troops
would capture eight Dutch bridges, thereby opening a pathway into Germany. Thirty-two thousand troops were to be dropped by parachute and
gliders behind enemy lines in three Dutch towns, the most important of
which was Arnhem. Two heavily armored SS Panzer divisions were sta-
tioned near Arnhem, but the Allies went ahead with their plan. Problems
ensued due to the lack of planes to carry out such a mission in one day as
well as the German antiaircraft defenses in the town, which forced the
Allies to make their drops miles away, thereby eliminating much of the
tactical surprise.

The battle of Arnhem, which turned out to be the largest Allied air
raid during World War II, began on September 17, 1944. Some of the
Germans who had lost their will to fight threw down their guns and ran,
which prompted celebration in the streets by townspeople, who showered
the Allied soldiers with flowers. But the party was, to say the least, premature. On the second day of Operation Market Garden, many airborne
troops were shot down by German artillery, and street battles ensued.
Fighting took place throughout Arnhem, including on the van Heemstra
property in suburban Oosterbeek. The attack was threatening to become
a failure. German tanks destroyed much of Arnhem, as thousands of Allied soldiers were killed and thousands more captured. An operation that
had appeared to secure the liberation of Arnhem two days earlier had
collapsed into an abysmal failure. While hiding in their cellar, Audrey
and her family could hear the gruesome sounds of Allied fighters being

burned or shot, while bombs exploded throughout the once-peaceful and picturesque town.

The van Heemstras were among the 90,000 Arnhem citizens who were ordered to evacuate. They moved to Audrey's grandfather's home in Velp, where they starved and shivered in a house with no food, no light, and no heat. They were forced to eat tulip bulbs to stay alive, while a stream of people who had been evacuated from their homes knocked on their door begging for food and shelter. About 40 did receive a place to stay for a while, but the lack of food forced them to continue their search elsewhere. The experience horrified Audrey, who tried to sleep through her hunger but was too weak even to climb the stairs to her bedroom. Her legs began to swell with edema, and she was suffering from jaundice. Ella feared that Audrey would die from hepatitis. A member of the Dutch underground relieved a bit of the hunger with a tin of food around Christmas, but soon that food was gone as well.

In March 1945, German soldiers with machine guns rounded up Audrey and a dozen other young women and ordered them to help staff their military kitchens. They were marched to German headquarters, which were poorly guarded. Though it has been debated whether Audrey ran home or escaped to spend the last month of the war in an abandoned cellar, all she had to do from that point was survive. And on May 5, 1945, the day after her 16th birthday, the sounds of gunfire and shelling were replaced by beautiful silence. She heard people singing, as the smell of English cigarettes wafted toward her. The family snuck upstairs, slowly pushed the front door open, and saw British troops surrounding the house. They had finally been liberated.

Audrey asked the soldiers for chocolate and was handed five bars of it. She devoured them all at once, which made her violently ill. But soon she and millions of others were to be fed far more nutritionally through the efforts of the United Nations Relief and Rehabilitation Administration (UNRRA), which was later transformed into the United Nations Children's Fund (UNICEF). Its selfless and tireless work feeding and clothing her starving, war-ravaged countrymen marked the beginning of Audrey's commitment to the organization. The UNRRA placed food, clothing, and basic medical supplies in local schools. Audrey picked out sweaters and skirts that had been shipped from the United States.

About three weeks later, to her great joy and relief, Alexander returned home to Arnhem after having emerged from his underground hideout. He showed up with his pregnant wife, who gave birth to Audrey's nephew Michael in mid-July. Soon thereafter, Ian also appeared at the front door after having walked most of the 325 miles from Berlin to Arnhem.

And what had become of her father? He and hundreds of other male pro-Nazi prisoners of the British government had been shipped off to a camp near Peel, which offered athletic and educational activities and conditions that were far from harsh. Hepburn-Ruston remained interned until April 1945 and was among the last of the detainees to be released. It would be decades before he would be heard from again.

Meanwhile, Audrey could now get on with her own life. But the terror and the hunger she experienced during World War II had changed her forever.

## NOTES

1. Maychick, Diana. *Audrey Hepburn: An Intimate Portrait* (New York: Carol), 1993), 27.

2. Barry Paris, *Audrey Hepburn* (New York: G. P. Putnam's Sons, 1996), 16.

3. Maychick, *Audrey Hepburn*, 29.

4. L. De Jong, *Lion Rampant: The Story of Holland's Resistance to the Nazis* (New York: Querido, 1943).

5. Donald Spoto, *Enchantment: The Life of Audrey Hepburn* (New York: Harmony Books, 2006), 23.

6. Paris, *Audrey Hepburn*, 24.

# Chapter 3

# BIRTH OF A CAREER

The freedom Audrey felt after the shooting had stopped was boundless. Her survival and that of her family brought tremendous relief and hope for the future. But the senseless brutality inflicted on the free people of the world by the Nazis would affect her profoundly for the rest of her life. She awoke in the middle of the night after having nightmares about torture. She tried in vain to rid herself of the gruesome thoughts about the war. Eventually, she came to grips with the fact that she could never fully escape it. What she had witnessed during World War II began to shape her philosophy on life, which is the way she was able to deal with it.

"I saw people die, I saw loved ones separated, I saw cruelty and hunger on a daily basis," she said. "All that proved to me is that nothing is more important than empathy for another human being's suffering. Nothing. Not a career, not wealth, not intelligence, certainly not status. We have to feel for one another if we're going to survive with dignity."[1]

Audrey's family indeed survived the war with dignity, and now it was time to celebrate their reunion and the love they felt for each other. They moved back to their little home in Arnhem, and in the summer of 1945, she volunteered at the Royal Military Invalids Home for injured and retired veterans in Bronbeek, a suburb of Arnhem. There she met a soldier named Terence Young, an aspiring film director who would, in the early 1960s, direct Audrey in the taut thriller *Wait until Dark*. A brigadier general named Mike Calvert was recovering in the next room, and when he heard that Young had designs on a career in film directing, he piqued Young's interest about doing a documentary on the September 1944 battle of Arnhem. Soon, Young and fellow director Brian Desmond

Hurst of Gaumont-British news were collaborating on a work titled *Men of Arnhem*, which has been lauded as one of the finest of all World War II documentaries. When Ella caught wind of the production, she eagerly introduced her daughter to the big shots at Gaumont-British in an attempt to further her career as a performer, but it only resulted in their suggestion that Audrey continue with her ballet lessons and the opinion that her mother was rather pushy.

Soon the family was looking for a new home and fresh start. Rotterdam had been destroyed by German bombing, so they grabbed the few valuable possessions that remained and moved to a small apartment in Amsterdam, where Ella landed a job as a cook for a middle-class family and continued plans to further her daughter's career. Audrey was still recovering from edema and hepatitis, so Ella believed reenrolling her in ballet classes would not only advance her professional aspirations, but also help her recover from her weakened state. Winja Marova had been so impressed with Audrey that she suggested that the 16-year-old study with one Sonia Gaskell, arguably the leading figure in Dutch ballet. Gaskell, a Lithuanian Jew who had escaped the Holocaust by going into hiding during the war, ran a school that later blossomed into the Dutch National Ballet. Her choreography was considered cutting edge at the time and was often set to modern jazz and Latin rhythms. Gaskell also prided herself in procuring premier young talent, including Audrey.

But despite her positive feelings toward her new student, Gaskell had doubts about her future as a ballet dancer. Though she believed Audrey to be technically flawless, she doubted such a gawky young woman could thrive. Audrey was tall, but with little muscle tone, particularly when she still weighed less than 100 pounds. Yet, despite Ella's inability to pay Gaskell anywhere near the going rate for her services, the prestigious instructor continued to give Audrey a chance and lauded her for her diligence and work ethic. In May 1946, Gaskell even paired Audrey with Beatrix Leoni, her top student, in an afternoon show at the Hortus Theater in Amsterdam. Audrey had picked up where she had left off before the war. She was driven toward a dancing career. While most of her female classmates danced merely for enjoyment and flirted with the boys who practiced with them, Audrey remained focused on the tasks at hand.

Music was her life. Audrey was overjoyed when Ella, who could barely scrape enough money together to pay for the essentials of life, bought her tickets for a season of performances given by the famed Amsterdam Concertgebouw Orchestra. Ella placed them strategically on the night table next to Audrey's bed on her 17th birthday. She also bought Audrey passes to a series of Beethoven string quartet concerts. Audrey couldn't even afford to take the trolley from her apartment to the concert hall, so she walked great distances to watch the performances.

Meanwhile, Audrey's ambitions as a dancer were placed on hold by the announcement in 1947 that Gaskell couldn't obtain the government funding necessary to continue to run her studio. Angry at the perception that the style of dance she taught played a role in her funding request being denied, Gaskell moved her business to Paris, where she believed she would find the freedom to choreograph and teach whatever form of modern dance she desired. That left her Dutch students out in the cold, but Audrey used the closure of the Gaskell dance studio as motivation to pursue a career in London. Coincidentally, a bilingual, British-Dutch travelogue was being produced in Amsterdam at the time and was being shot in several locations throughout the country. Dutch director Huguenot van der Linden was searching for a Dutch girl who could play an airline hostess who would open and close the short film. A friend told van der Linden about Audrey, who was called in for an audition. She would prove to be the last candidate the director needed to see.

"I stared at [Audrey] while she was chirping away about her ballet work, and then I picked up the telephone and told my partner to stop looking for a girl, since she had just walked in," van der Linden recalled. "I remember saying, 'Did you ever see a dream walking? Well, I did.' Audrey was bright, cheerful and chummy and just emanated style, breeding, intelligence and good manners. She was wonderful. Her part took only three or four days to shoot. I tried to make another film with her, but I couldn't find the money."[2]

Audrey was hired on the spot. The taste of show business had her yearning for more, but the ballet remained in her blood. She and Ella moved to London in 1948 with the equivalent of 10 dollars between them, which they spent immediately on the advance rent for a room in a boarding house. Britain was foundering economically; its recovery from war was coming along much slower than in the Netherlands. Ella tried in vain to recover the money and estate she had lost during the war and was forced to take a job in a florist shop that paid 10 dollars a week, while Audrey did clerical work during the day and also did some modeling for magazine ads hawking such items as soap and shampoo.

In the meantime, Audrey auditioned for a spot in a ballet school run by the legendary and disciplined Marie Rambert, who had been known to punish students who slouched or folded their arms by smacking them in the knuckles with a stick. Then 60 years old, Rambert had founded the companies that would eventually evolve into Sadler's Wells and the Royal Ballet. Though she questioned Audrey's potential as a ballet dancer, she

felt a sense of pity and provided her with a scholarship and even housed
and fed her for six months. Audrey quickly realized that she was far behind
Rambert's other students, many of whom had continued to take lessons
throughout the war and enjoyed five additional years of experience. After
all, the Germans had bombed London but had never goose-stepped into
it. She also became self-conscious about her height, which was considered
a drawback in ballet dancing.

Audrey's early years in London were the only time in her postwar
life that she displayed a prodigious appetite, which was unleashed after
five years of virtual starvation. She would devour whole jars of jam in one
sitting. Audrey gained 20 pounds but lost it all through hard work and
a determination to excel on the dance floor. She abstained from eating
sweets and starches, which allowed her to quickly shed weight that never
appeared again. But in the end, fewer pounds couldn't make up for lack
of experience. As the summer of 1948 drew to a close, Madame Rambert announced that she was taking several of her dancers on a 15-month
tour of Australia and New Zealand. She explained that Audrey was not
among them for reasons ranging from too much height to too little training. Though crestfallen, Audrey, in retrospect, understood the decision
that for all intents ended her dreams of a career in ballet.

"My technique didn't compare with that of the girls who had five years
of Sadler's Wells teaching, paid by their families, and who had always had
good food and bomb shelters," Audrey said. "Reason made me see that I
just couldn't be so square as to go on studying ballet."[3]

Instead, Audrey, who moved back with her mother in October 1948,
accompanied several other shunned students and began visiting the offices of producers and agents in search of acting roles. She quickly landed
a spot in an American musical stage comedy titled *High Button Shoes*,
slated for production in London. Audrey was among the last of 40 girls selected from 3,000 candidates to sing and dance in a chorus line of bathing
beauties racing around to wacky songs intended to bring back memories
of silent films. Audrey received 32 dollars a week for her efforts. The show
opened just before Christmas and was generally very well received, boast-
ing a commendable run of 291 performances.

While she remained unmentioned in the reviews, London producer
Cecil Landeau did notice her and offered her a spot in a lively musical
revue titled *Sauce Tartare* in May 1949. That show would provide Audrey
more of a spotlight as one of just five dancers and a few lines in some of
the 27 sketches. She worked a whirlwind schedule of six evening and two
matinee performances a day and squeezing in more modeling for magazine
and newspaper advertisements to boot. Audrey played various roles in

*Sauce Tartare,* including a shop girl and a classical dancer, and began to receive notice. Fashion photographer Anthony Beauchamp compared her to such movie stars as Vivien Leigh and Greta Garbo. "[I] had the feeling of making a true discovery when I found her," he said. "She had such freshness and a kind of spiritual beauty."[4]

The production was a smash. It ran for 433 performances at Cambridge Square and featured performers for whom Landau had scoured the earth. It spurred Landeau to follow up with *Sauce Piquante* and return Audrey to the stage in a larger role at about 65 dollars a week. Among her bits was to walk across stage in a French maid outfit, holding up a card to announce each new skit. Audrey also landed speaking parts in several comedy sketches. Despite her petite figure, she was being noticed for her beauty and charm, much to the dismay of more than one of her colleagues. "I can't stand it," roared busty dancer Aud Johanssen. "I've got the best [breasts] on stage, and yet they're all staring at a girl who hasn't got any."[5]

Another source of resentment revolved around Audrey's comparatively weak dancing. *Sauce Piquante* featured some of the premier dancers in Britain, and it was apparent to any expert that Audrey was too stiff and inexperienced to be among them, yet her attractive personality drew praise. Despite being surrounded by many stars of the show, Audrey always received the most thunderous ovation.

Audrey experienced something else from performing in *Sauce Piquante*— her first boyfriend. She began dating handsome French singer and lyricist Marcel le Bon, who presented roses to her in her dressing room every night. She later insisted she was more appreciative of his kindness and attention than infatuated by him, but Landeau was infuriated by reports in the tabloids that she and le Bon were planning to wed. After all, he had actually placed a no-marriage clause in her contract for fear that such an occurrence would steal publicity away from the show. Ella also feared a union between le Bon and her daughter. After all, she didn't want any romance to slow down Audrey's career, which was just starting to gather steam. Landeau, however, was taking no chances. The vindictive producer had opened a new revue titled *Summer Nights* that was to feature le Bon, but he fired the Frenchman even before the first curtain was raised on opening night.

Encouraged by her successes, Audrey began taking her craft quite seriously. She started to take acting lessons with British character actor Felix Aylmer. The relationship was much like the one featuring Professor Higgins and her own character of Eliza Doolittle in the hit musical *My Fair Lady,* though Audrey's aristocratic background gave her little in common with the flower girl in that wildly popular film. Aylmer did, however, teach her proper English diction as well as nuances of acting such as using stillness and responsiveness in scenes in drawing the audience to her, even when she was doing nothing in a particular scene. Aylmer had gained quite a reputation as an acting teacher, having also furthered the careers of luminaries such as Vivien Leigh and Charles Laughton. And Audrey certainly needed to learn about serious acting—she had seen very few films in her life.

Her relationship with Aylmer brought further benefits. The former Shakespearean actor had connections and was not averse to furthering the careers of the students he deemed particularly talented. Aylmer set up a screen test for Audrey for an epic Hollywood religious film titled *Quo Vadis*. Director Mervyn LeRoy was impressed with Audrey, but the studio (Metro-Goldwyn-Mayer) rejected her after a brief look at her test, opting instead for the better-known Deborah Kerr. Audrey was facing a bit of a chicken-egg problem—film producers rejected Audrey because they sought stars for their movies, but she couldn't become a star until given an opportunity. Meanwhile, she was barely making enough money to support herself and her by then unemployed mother.

Enter Robert Lennard, casting director at Associated British Pictures Corporation (ABPC). The company, which had been saved financially by Jack Warner of Warner Bros. fame in 1950, owned Elstree Studios in Hertfordshire. Lennard offered Audrey a three-picture contract that would pay her between 1,000 and 3,000 dollars per film, which seemed like a king's ransom for a performer whose most recent work had brought her less than 25 dollars a week. But though she was finally able to pay her bills without concern, Audrey received little satisfaction from the miniscule roles and the characters she was given to portray.

She appeared for a mere 20 seconds and spoke one line in the first film, the poorly received *One Wild Oat*, in which she played a hotel receptionist who takes a phone call from her married boyfriend. Another bit part as a nightclub cigarette girl awaited Audrey in *Laughter in Paradise*, which required little rehearsal and shooting time. The third film was the highly successful Alec Guinness comedy *The Lavender Hill Mob*, in which Audrey appeared briefly in a South American restaurant as Chiquita, one of the main character's love interests. The last movie was named top film of 1951 by the British Film Academy, but Audrey received little attention.

Though dissatisfied with all three roles, Audrey certainly couldn't afford to turn down the paychecks, so she signed another contract with ABPC for three more films with slightly larger roles and an income escalating to 5,000 dollars per film. She was featured in seven scenes as a young wife in *Young Wives' Tale*, a risqué farce about couples sharing homes in postwar England. Audrey portrayed a paranoid young woman who feared that all men were out to harm her. She suffered through the entire filmmaking process, including from her relationship with director Henry Cass, who lambasted her for every aspect of her performance and was particularly critical of her exaggerated English accent, which he compared unfavorably to the speaking talents of the more established actors in the movie. "[Cass] had it in for me," Audrey complained. "It was the only unhappy experience I ever had making a picture."[6]

The unhappiness in her professional life was tempered by the happiness in her personal life revolving around new boyfriend James Hanson, a 28-year-old millionaire socialite whose family ran a trucking business in Yorkshire. Hanson, who had been a notorious playboy and had counted among his previous girlfriends such movie stars as Jean Simmons, Ava Gardner, and Joan Collins, had served gallantly during World War II and was now spending his time fox hunting and yachting. A trustee of the D'Oyly Carte opera company, Hanson met Audrey at a cocktail party and felt an immediate attraction. He invited her to lunch the following day, after which the relationship blossomed. Audrey not only felt strongly about Hanson, but considering that her career as an actor remained questionable, she was drawn to the sense of security the relationship brought.

Audrey, however, was torn by what appeared to be two distinctly separate paths from which she now must choose. She could draw closer to Hanson as well as his friends and lifestyle, thereby eliminating any financial need for an acting career. Or she could continue to pursue her chosen profession, which could very well disillusion Hanson and place their relationship in jeopardy. Though many believe Ella was strongly opposed to Audrey's growing feelings for and dependence on Hanson for those very reasons, Hanson later insisted otherwise. "[Ella] was always very encouraging about me with Audrey," he said. "She felt the age difference—about six years—was right and that somebody in a solid business was right for somebody on the artistic side. She would be marrying somebody with his feet on the ground, not in show business, with all its uncertainties."[7]

Hanson claimed that not only did Ella believe he was well suited to marry her daughter, but that he had also worked out an agreement with Audrey and Ella that the former would make one movie a year, with an option to perform in one play as well. He added that the rather limited schedule was a result of Audrey's desire to spent a great deal of time with him as his wife.

Audrey, however, claimed otherwise. She was swept off her feet by Hanson's love and romantic gestures, such as open displays of affection and his presenting her such gifts as flowers, perfume, and Swiss chocolates, but she was not about to jeopardize her career for him.

"I loved the idea of finding a partner," she said. "But it was just that: an idea. As soon as it became clear that I would have to give up the artistic and cultural life of London for an existence talking about golf and hunting and fishing, I was no longer anxious to get married."[8]

If Audrey indeed yearned to maximize her acting career and believed furthering her relationship with Hanson was counterproductive to reaching that goal, her next film certainly increased those fears, while giving her a reason for optimism about her future in show business. She was about to receive her first big break in the movie *Secret People*, which was directed by Thorold Dickinson, who had been thoroughly impressed with Audrey in *Sauce Piquante* and had kept her in mind for future roles. A taut, rather depressing film about the political intrigue gripping Europe before World War II, *Secret People* offered far greater and vastly different opportunities for Audrey than did the fluffy comedies in which she had been rather briefly appearing.

There was a catch, however. Audrey, who was to be in a supporting role as Nora Brentano, was on the brink of earning an opportunity not only to act alongside established European stars, but also to dance in two ballet sequences. At first, the producers felt she was too tall in comparison to the leading men in the film, which nearly cost her the role. In late February 1951, however, she was deemed far too talented for such a triviality to prevent her from playing Nora. The 21-year-old had earned the most important role of her young career—that of a beautiful ballet student who flees from London along with her sister after a central European dictator murders their father. Nora is soon drawn into an assassination plot against the killer. The role allowed Audrey to display her understated exuberance and ability to show emotions such as grief, anxiety, or dismay by the slightest movement or change of expression. They were to be her trademarks for years to come.

Audrey's most challenging scene revolved around a conversation between Nora and her sister after a bomb explosion killed several guests at a party at which the former had been dancing. As she rehearsed the scene, her thoughts rushed back to her experiences during the war in Arnhem. She initially froze as her lines were to be delivered, but Dickinson suggested she use those memories to feel the emotions behind her words. Audrey retired to the corner of the set and focused her mind on her experiences during the war. She blocked out all distraction and thought about her fellow Dutchmen being killed by bombs and her brother being carted away by the Nazis. Audrey returned to the set with tears welling up in her eyes. The pain she felt allowed her to deliver her lines with power and eloquence.

During the filming, Audrey developed a friendship with Italian actress Valentina Cortese, who starred as her sister Maria. Audrey not only learned some of the finer points of acting from Cortese, but also soaked in a bit of advice about media and public attention as it relates to the personal life of an actor. Cortese offered to her young friend that closeness with reporters and fans had its place but was also likely to destroy an actor's private existence. Cortese warned Audrey that the attention was particularly suffocating in Hollywood. The veteran actor then spoke directly to Audrey. "Think hard before you sign a long-term contract, dear," Cortese told her. "Liberty is the most wonderful thing of all."[9]

Though *Secret People* failed to find the critical acclaim Dickinson had hoped, Audrey was widely praised. Her performance motivated the powers-that-be to place her name just below those of costars Cortese and Serge Reggiani in the credits. But she didn't feel she had yet earned the attention she was about to receive from the media and was annoyed by much of it, including questions about her budding romance with James Hanson. She agreed to participate in a layout for the magazine *Illustrated*, for which she was required to spend her day in the Sussex countryside feeding ducks in a village pond, paddling a boat with her bare feet, and strolling along the hills. She expressed fear over such attention to director Lindsay Anderson, who was present at the photo shoot. "I'm worried [the public] will get sick of hearing about me," Audrey said. "I'd much rather wait until I have something to show. Instead of risking a tremendous anticlimax when people finally do see the first little bits of films."[10]

The next little bit of film in which she agreed to appear was *Monte Carlo Baby*, in which she played a movie star chasing a lost baby. Audrey later admitted that she took the role in that widely panned comedy for such reasons as the Dior dress she would wear in the movie that she would be allowed to keep, the fact that it would be shot on the French Riviera, and that her mother, who had been feeling a bit blue over her daughter's continued relationship with James Hanson, needed a vacation. But as she rehearsed one scene during the filming of *Monte Carlo Baby*, she noticed an elderly woman in a wheelchair watching her intently.

That stranger who had her eye on the young actress was none other than beloved French novelist Colette. Audrey's life was once again about to change.

# NOTES

1. Diana Maychick, *Audrey Hepburn: An Intimate Portrait* (New York: Carol, 1993), 47.

   2. Charles Higham, *Audrey: The Life of Audrey Hepburn* (New York: Macmillan, 1984), 24–25.

   3. Donald Spoto, *Enchantment: The Life of Audrey Hepburn* (New York: Harmony Books, 2006), 40.

   4. Ibid., 42.

   5. Barry Paris, *Audrey Hepburn* (New York: G. P. Putnam's Sons, 1996), 45.

   6. Spoto, *Enchantment*, 50.

   7. Paris, *Audrey Hepburn*, 53.

   8. Maychick, *Audrey Hepburn*, 65.

   9. Spoto, *Enchantment*, 53.

   10. Higham, *Audrey*, 38.

# Chapter 4

# FROM CIGARETTE GIRL
# TO STARDOM

The commotion caused by the entrance of Colette on the set interrupted the rehearsal for *Monte Carlo Baby*. Director Jean Boyer, who had yet to notice who had been the "showstopper," wheeled around in anger, until he discovered it had been the famous novelist. He was honored when Colette asked him if she could watch the scene being shot. She and her husband, fellow writer Maurice Goudaket, were placed behind the camera, where they gazed on silently. Colette peered at Audrey's performance with fascination. The feeling was mutual. Audrey, who had read and thoroughly enjoyed all her works, felt self-conscious as she delivered the silly lines from what she knew to be a horrible script in front of the literary legend.

Colette requested the audience of a crew member, whom she asked the name of the actor she had been studying. She was told it was Audrey and that her mother represented the young woman. Ella was excited by the honor of speaking with Colette, and then became overwhelmed when informed by the novelist that her daughter was ideal for the role of Gigi in a forthcoming Broadway production, adapted from Colette's novel of the same name. Colette explained to Ella that Gigi was a young Parisian trained by her worldly grandmother and aunt about the finer things in life.

Ella would have preferred to agree at that very moment. But her judgment was tempered by such considerations as Audrey's current contract with Associated British Pictures as well as her daughter's own thoughts. They continued their discussion in Colette's hotel suite, whereupon Audrey was summoned into the room. Deeply flattered, she nevertheless blurted out that she didn't feel ready for Broadway or the trappings of stardom. Audrey returned to the set, but neither Colette nor her husband was about to accept defeat. Goudaket wired Anita Loos, who had been asked to streamline the play, and flat out claimed that Audrey would not only be perfect for the role, but that she was also willing to play the part. He invited Loos and producer Gilbert Miller to see Audrey in London. "She is greatly thought of by the film people generally and considered a future star of the first magnitude," Goudaket added. "I believe, however, that she has had little experience on the stage. She is very pretty and has that piquant quality necessary for the part."[1]

But did Audrey want the part? Soon she was in a safe place—the waiting arms of James Hanson, who whisked her off to a weekend in the country. She believed not only that she wasn't a seasoned enough actor to accept the role of Gigi, but also that the relationship with Hanson would suffer if she was performing in New York. Though it has been speculated that Hanson wanted to marry Audrey and had encouraged her to give up her career, it is certain that she remained emotionally tied to him and was frightened at the prospect of being an ocean apart.

Audrey agreed to meet with Loos and Miller, who was tremendously wealthy and an imposing figure at 280 pounds. Arguably the most powerful Broadway producer of his era, he financed his own plays. His first encounter with Audrey was merely to get acquainted, but he was taken enough by her personality to schedule a reading for Loos and himself the following day. Though unimpressed with Audrey's audition and concerned about her lack of voice projection (theater actors were not miked in those days), they understood how much landing the young actor meant to Colette and simply planned on having veteran stage actor Cathleen Nesbitt coach her at her country home just outside New York City. By that time, the encouragement from Colette had Audrey warming up to the idea, despite the fact that her marriage to Hanson would certainly have to be postponed. Though still lacking confidence in her ability to handle a starring role in a Broadway play, her doubts were overtaken by flattery and anticipation.

Suddenly, however, she was the actor of the hour. Audrey became a sought-after commodity, which threatened to throw a monkey wrench in her plans. While Miller worked with Associated British Pictures to extricate her from a commitment to appear in additional films, she was discovered by acclaimed Hollywood director William Wyler, who was looking for a lead actor for the Paramount film *Roman Holiday*. The role was that of a restless princess in Rome on official business who escapes from her entourage and meets a newspaper journalist (played by established star

Gregory Peck) who was in the Italian capital to write a story about her
and eventually falls in love with her. Audrey was contacted by Paramount
to test for the part, which added another agonizing decision she would
be forced to make. How could she accept the role in *Roman Holiday* if
*Gigi* enjoyed a long run? And when, pray tell, would she ever find time to
marry the man she loved? Miller encouraged her to turn down the offer
to test for the romantic comedy for fear that she might be motivated to
back out of *Gigi*.

Audrey, however, agreed to a screen test for *Roman Holiday*. Wyler
placed Thorold Dickinson, who had directed her in *Secret People*, in charge
of the test. Dickinson formulated a plan that was kept secret from Audrey,
in which the cameras would continue rolling well after her lines had been
delivered so the powers that be could soak in her personality. After speaking her part, she enthusiastically and without a trace of pretentiousness
asked for a response to her performance, then spoke sweetly to Dickinson
and the camera crew. Her vulnerability was evident, and though she still
lacked a grasp of the nuances of acting, she projected herself as driven
to maximize her talent. Audrey was asked to change back to her street
clothes and have a conversation with Dickinson but was again unaware
that the film continued to roll in the camera. Her sincerity during that
chat also impressed Dickinson, who rushed the film of the screen test and
posttest to Wyler in Hollywood.

Duly impressed, Paramount sent a contract to Audrey, offering her an
opportunity to appear in seven movies in seven years with a year off between each, but she balked at the long commitment, opting instead for a
two-year deal that also allowed her to pursue work on stage and in television. It was believed at Paramount that *Gigi* would last two months at the
most, which would allow the filming of *Roman Holiday* to be completed in
1952, before the sizzling Italian summer set in. With her mother close by,
Audrey signed the contract and simultaneously became the youngest actor
ever to have committed to a leading role in both film and on Broadway.

That commitment to her career translated into a lack of commitment
to her fiancé—at least in his mind. Audrey was having second thoughts
about the relationship, especially considering that Hanson apparently
thought little enough about her professional future to object to such opportunities of a lifetime as starring in a Hollywood movie and on Broadway. And, frankly, she was no longer certain she was ready for marriage,
though she also wanted to maintain the relationship.

"It's interesting that the only person objecting was the man I was supposed to marry," Audrey said. "I guess even subconsciously, as much as
I wanted to go along with him on the surface of things, I had to face the

fact that part of me wanted to try this exciting thing. It would be an adventure, it would mean financial reward, and I would be forced to come out of my shell a little. Plus, and this is hard to admit, I could use it to postpone the wedding."[2]

Soon Audrey was embarking on an 18-day excursion to New York. The uneasiness she felt was not a result of the ship rolling over the waves, but rather a lack of confidence in her ability to act in a starring role on Broadway. But she also experienced a sense of excitement as she passed the Statue of Liberty, docked at 3:00 A.M., and saw the Manhattan skyline lit up in its entire splendor. She was greeted by one of Miller's representatives and whisked away to watch the New York Yankees clinch the 1951 World Series title at Yankee Stadium, where she got caught up in the cheering without the slightest understanding of baseball.

After spending a day becoming acclimated to New York, she visited Miller, who was alarmed at the 15 pounds Audrey had gained gorging herself on chocolate during her trip. She was no longer the diminutive figure he had grown to adore in London. He dispatched her to Dinty Moore's restaurant and gave the owner strict orders—serve Audrey nothing but steak tartare for a week. The plan had its desired result. And it would be the last time Audrey ever attempted or needed to shed weight.

Meanwhile, Audrey toiled daily on increasing voice range and projection at the country home of Cathleen Nesbitt, who would escort her to the garden, where she would be instructed to whisper, shout, and speak at every level in between. The veteran actor then escorted Audrey to the rehearsal hall to test her amplification, which remained weak but was acceptable. Audrey would never be hailed for a strong voice at any point in her career, but it became apparent from the start that she could command an audience. Her natural vulnerability and insecurity resulted in a projection of humility that audiences found sweet and refreshing.

But was she experienced and talented enough to take the role of Gigi and run with it? Miller had his doubts after several days of rehearsal. She lacked the ability to properly phrase her lines, which led him to begin searching for possible replacements. She became exaggerated in her movements. If the script called for her to laugh, she would do so hysterically. Miller had asked her to be animated, but she went overboard. In fact, according to Miller's assistant Morrie Gottleib, his boss actually fired Audrey on more than one occasion, only to reel her back in.

"Miller fired her [after five days of rehearsals]," Gottleib said. "By the next morning, he realized that it was too late to replace her, so he gave her another chance, and then he fired her a few days later. This went on up to opening night. Poor Audrey was on the verge of a nervous collapse."[3]

Outside factors also contributed to her emotional anxieties. She missed both her mother and her fiancé, particularly after one evening in her hotel room following rehearsal, during which a suicidal guest jumped from the 18th floor, bounced off her windowsill, and plunged to his death. Badly shaken, Audrey pounded on the door across the hall and was greeted by emerging young actor David Niven and his wife, who talked her through her distress.

Her initial working relationship with director Raymond Rouleau proved far from soothing. Audrey was attempting to play the part of a girl blossoming into a confident woman, but she herself had yet to make the same transformation. Rouleau, who had earned a reputation as an impatient and nervous man, often screamed at Audrey for her awkward performance and delivery of her lines. Rouleau's widow later communicated to biographer Charles Higham that the first week of rehearsals was particularly disastrous. "The first eight days of work with Audrey were truly terrible; Audrey had no idea what she was doing," she wrote. "She was acting extremely badly, totally failing to understand the meaning of the text, going out late at night and arriving tired at the theater in the mornings."[4]

Rouleau's widow added that her quite disturbed late husband summoned Audrey for a private meeting and told her frankly that if she didn't dedicate herself to proper work, sleep, and eating habits, he would decline all responsibility for her future on Broadway and in *Gigi*. She wrote that Audrey not only performed far better after the confrontation, but her relationship with Rouleau also improved dramatically.

Among the bits of advice she took to heart concerned her diet. The crash diet suggested by Miller after she had arrived in New York landed her at 100 pounds and made her weak and lightheaded. Among those who detected a problem was Miller's wife, Kitty. She took the terrified young actor to lunch and fed her steak, which Audrey admitted gave her strength. Audrey later offered her belief that she had starved as a self-punishment for performing so poorly on stage, but putting some solid food in her stomach made her less critical of herself, strengthened her concentration, and allowed her to act with greater confidence and less nervousness.

The media hype leading up to the opening of *Gigi*, however, would have had even the coolest veteran actor a bit apprehensive. Some newspaper reviewers predicted Audrey would take America by storm. The praise she received after a two-week preview run in Philadelphia at the Walnut Street Theater, the oldest playhouse in the United States, gave Audrey confidence, but also served to heighten expectations when the show opened in New York's Fulton Theater on November 24, 1951.

She needn't have worried. Though nearly frozen with terror and stricken with a cold, Audrey performed brilliantly that evening. She forgot a few lines in the last scene, but it mattered little because she had already won over the critics and the audience. Though reviews of the play were mixed, those of the 22-year-old actress were unanimous. They praised her to the skies.

"[She] is a young actress of charm, honesty and talent who ought to be interned in America and trapped into appearing in a fine play," wrote *New York Times* critic Brooks Atkinson. "[She] is the one fresh element in the performance. She is an actress, and as Gigi, she develops a full-length character from artless gaucheries in the first act to a stirring climax in the last scene. It is a fine piece of sustained acting that is spontaneous, lucid and captivating."[5] Chimed in influential critic Richard Watts Jr. of the *New York Post*, "The delightful Miss Hepburn obviously is not an experienced actress. But her quality is so winning and so right that she is the success of the evening....Miss Hepburn is as fresh and frisky as a puppy out of a tub. She brings a candid innocence and a tomboy intelligence to a part that might have gone sticky, and her performance comes as a breath of fresh air in a stifling season."[6]

Miller was certainly convinced. A week after opening night, he had her name placed above the title on the marquee outside the theater. She posed for the media as photographers flashed their cameras while she placed the last lightbulb on the last letter of her last name. Autograph seekers surrounded her after every performance. Stars of the entertainment world would seek her company. The praise and attention still couldn't bring her confidence, but that very timidity and self-doubt had already become her most attractive features. Her son Sean understood that as well as anyone. "She was basically a very insecure person whose very insecurity made everyone fall in love with her," he wrote. "[She was] a star who couldn't see her own light."[7]

James Hanson could certainly see the light. He paid her a surprise three-day visit in time for the premiere, during which time they formalized their engagement. No longer suggesting that she give up her acting career, Audrey's fiancé also flew in from his Canadian office to spend time with her during the holiday season. He had her moved from the rather ordinary Blackstone Hotel to the swank Waldorf Towers and placed Ella, who had also paid a visit, on the same floor. The couple planned on marrying between the end of the *Gigi* run and the start of shooting for *Roman Holiday* in Rome, then on settling down in Huddersfield.

While Hanson was whisking Audrey around New York, she developed a highly beneficial personal and professional relationship with Nesbitt, who played the role of her aunt in *Gigi*. The seasoned actor proved to be both a mentor and a friend. She was quite the fan of Audrey, in whose talent she believed more than did Audrey herself. While others, such as Rouleau, displayed impatience and a quick temper with the young actor, Nesbitt proved to be an understanding and energetic teacher. She would remain Audrey's fast friend until her death in 1982, at the age of 93.

And as *Gigi* played to packed houses, Audrey continued to receive critical acclaim and achieve stardom. *Life* magazine produced a full-page story and photo spread, while rival *Look* also ran a highly complimentary feature. Her honesty and genuine personality, praised by audiences and critics, were also noted by those who met Audrey in person during the many festivities in her honor. Executives in the entertainment industry tripped all over themselves in attempts to sign Audrey, but her commitment to *Gigi* and *Roman Holiday* precluded her from testing too many waters.

And her personal life? What personal life? As *Gigi* continued to capture the imagination of theater aficionados and the publicity machine began to hype *Roman Holiday*, she rarely enjoyed a moment to herself. It seemed everyone wanted a piece of the timid new star with the waiflike look. She was the guest of honor at dozens of functions, where it was discovered that the public was as taken with her personally as they were with her on stage. Even the wealthiest New York socialites clamored to catch a glimpse of her. Audrey couldn't have possibly kept pace with all the interview and photo requests, many of which she was never informed about. Gilbert Miller and his publicists spent much of their time fielding and rejecting such inquiries.

One medium in which Audrey did dabble was television, which was rapidly gaining in popularity and public demand during the early 1950s. As a means to further publicize *Gigi* in February 1952, she accepted a brief dramatic appearance as Lady Jane Grey in the play *Nine Days a Queen* on the variety show *Toast of the Town*, hosted by future TV icon Ed Sullivan. Two months later, she played a crippled 16-year-old with designs on a dancing career in Hollywood in *Rainy Day in Paradise Junction*. The sad and serious role allowed her to expand her horizons as an actor.

The unexpectedly long run of *Gigi* forced Paramount to postpone *Roman Holiday*, but only for a short while. Despite the fact that the play continued to sell out, Audrey's contract expired, and Miller's agreement with Paramount required him to shut down his production in May. Miller was assured, however, that Audrey would be available for a national tour of *Gigi* in the fall. She desperately yearned for time off for reasons that included a wedding and honeymoon with James Hanson, but her professional obligations wouldn't allow it. She did manage to get away with him for a short vacation in Paris, but soon she was hightailing it to Rome to start filming *Roman Holiday*. And it came as no surprise that the Italian media and star-seekers mobbed her the moment she stepped off the plane.

Audrey's enthusiasm for the film had been heightened by the opportunity to work with Edith Head, the premier clothing designer in Hollywood. Head had been dispatched to New York to discuss what the character Princess Ann might wear. Audrey was always thrilled to talk about wardrobe, and she welcomed any break from the rigors of her stage work at the time. Head, who quickly developed a rapport with Audrey that would lead to a lifelong friendship, appreciated that she was about to work with a woman who boasted a strong sense of fashion and understood how to accentuate and show off her slender figure. Audrey was not fearful to change Head's sketches, adding simpler necklines, wider belts, and flatter shoes. Though timid in some matters, such was not the case in matters of wardrobe. Every designer would eventually become well aware that she would wear nothing that she hadn't approved—and only after significant alterations.

Soon Audrey met costar Gregory Peck, who, at 36 years old, was at the peak of his career. Peck had initially rejected the role, just as William Wyler's first choice, Cary Grant, had, because of his impression after watching Audrey's screen test that the princess was the star of the film. But Wyler talked Peck into accepting the role of the reporter by appealing to his sense of pride and exclaiming to Peck that he was not the kind of actor to judge a part by its size. The speech was so effective that soon Peck was on the phone with agent George Chasin, requesting that Audrey receive equal billing. "We all knew that [Audrey] was going to be an important star," Peck said, "and we began to talk off-camera about the chance that she might win an Academy Award in her first film."[8]

The soon-to-be movie couple met at an introductory party at the Excelsior Hotel. Peck approached her with right arm extended and, in a mocking reference to their upcoming roles, exclaimed, "Your Royal Highness." She replied, "I hope I don't let you down."[9] That meeting was enough for tabloid writers, who immediately began reporting with nary a shred of evidence that the *Roman Holiday* costars had become romantically involved. Paramount did nothing to quell the rumors, figuring the publicity would only prove beneficial.

What did prove beneficial was Audrey's professional relationship with Peck. She appreciated how both he and Wyler made her feel at ease through their relaxed styles. There was none of the pettiness between the actors and director during the filming of *Roman Holiday* that she had experienced in working in her previous movies. Positive personal relationships were required because tempers could have very well been short in the stifling heat and humidity. The summer of 1952 had been one of the hottest on record in Rome, and it had shown no signs of cooling off into September— the temperatures generally exceeded 90 degrees. And the temperatures weren't all that were rising: political tensions were heightened as Fascists and Communists battled in the streets. At one point, several bundles of explosives were found under a bridge over the Tiber River, where filming was about to take place.

Filming during the height of the vacation season also proved difficult as both tourists and local residents, caught up in the excitement of witnessing an on-location movie, which was rare in those days, often got in the way. Many of them hoped to catch a glimpse of Peck, the only established star in the film. But he was later to claim that watching Audrey flit about the set provided him with the most joyful moviemaking of his career.

The part of a sheltered princess tasting the simple pleasures of life for the first time proved ideal for Audrey. She gave the role a vitality and freshness that led one to believe that she, too, was experiencing the same sense of freedom. Her ability to convey the thrill and satisfaction of a princess not being recognized showed that she was maturing as an actor. She struggled, at times, at bringing out the strong emotional feelings in her role, including in one of the final scenes, a touching moment in which she must part from the journalist and return to her life of royal captivity. Audrey was required to shed tears of sorrow but held up the works as she continued to fail. Finally, Wyler, who had been a model of sweetness and patience throughout the filming, screamed at her with such harshness that she burst into tears, whereupon the scene was successfully shot. Audrey was forever grateful to Wyler for helping her grow as an actor.

Both Audrey and *Roman Holiday* were to become tremendous successes. Her professional and personal lives were about to change dramatically.

## NOTES

1. Charles Higham, *Audrey: The Life of Audrey Hepburn* (New York: Macmillan, 1984), 41.

2. Diana Maychick, *Audrey Hepburn: An Intimate Portrait* (New York: Carol, 1993), 79.

3. Barry Paris, *Audrey Hepburn* (New York: G. P. Putnam's Sons, 1996), 68–69.

4. Higham, *Audrey*, 48.

5. Brooks Atkinson, *New York Times*, November 26, 1951, 20. Article title unavailable.

6. Richard Watts Jr., *New York Post*, November 26, 1951. Article title unavailable.

7. Sean Hepburn Ferrer, *Audrey Hepburn: An Elegant Spirit* (New York: Atria Books, 2003), 209.

8. Paris, *Audrey Hepburn*, 78.

9. Alexander Walker, *Audrey: Her Real Story* (New York: St. Martin's Griffin, 1994), 70.

# Chapter 5

# MOVIES OVER MARRIAGE

*Roman Holiday* has been described as Cinderella in reverse—a movie about a princess who yearns for an ordinary existence—but blossoming as an actor and receiving praise for her work made Audrey feel like a princess. It also cemented her career choice and altered her priorities. Despite her strong feelings for James Hanson and his devotion and passion for her, she could no longer justify setting a date and settling down at that point in her life, which had become a whirlwind of professional success and activity. She understood that as soon as her work on *Roman Holiday* was completed in September 1952 (it would not be released until August 1953), she was obligated to take *Gigi* on the road for a long American tour that included stops in Baltimore, Pittsburgh, Boston, Cleveland, Cincinnati, Chicago, Detroit, Washington, San Francisco, and Los Angeles.

Audrey and her fiancé had planned to wed on September 30. They had invited 200 friends and family members to the ceremony, which was set for a parish church in Huddersfield and was to be the event of the year in that town. But as the date drew closer, her love for Hanson diminished. Rather than giddiness and excitement over the wedding, she felt only a romantic obligation to a man who flew to Rome as often as possible to be with her and had shown only love and caring for her.

Whether Hanson sensed a problem or simply feared Audrey wouldn't have time between her professional obligations for a wedding is up to conjecture. But on July 8, he penned a letter to Paramount executive producer Henry Henigson, requesting a conclusion of his fiancée's commitment to the picture by early September, though he strangely did not mention the wedding. By early August, the delays often associated with filmmaking pushed the complete date back to September 25, which further panicked Hanson. He again wrote Henigson on August 12, this time specifying that Audrey needed to be released from her duties in mid-September so she could be married and return to New York in time to tour with *Gigi*. Soon thereafter, he issued a press release announcing their wedding date of September 30. Paramount showered her with gifts, including her wardrobe and accessories from the film, but Audrey quickly declared that the engagement had been aborted. Despite Hanson's strong desire to wed, the relationship ended amicably. But he contradicted anyone who accused him of stifling her career in favor of marriage.

"Had she married me, Audrey would have continued with her career," he said. "No doubt about it. I believed in that. There was never any 'either/ or' [marriage/career] problem. She was somebody whose star and whose destiny had been set by her talent. It would have been pointless to try to persuade her to do anything else....I loved Audrey very much. I've not loved very many women in my life in that way. Yet I have no regrets whatsoever about her decision."[1]

Though Hanson spent Christmas with Audrey in Chicago, her current spot on the *Gigi* tour, the handwriting was on the wall. By the time he departed, it had become apparent that they would never again be anything more than friends. Her love life continued to be a source of media speculation after the *Gigi* road show ended on May 16, 1953, and as the release of *Roman Holiday* approached. But her romantic situation after her shattered relationship drew parallels to the loneliness of Princess Ann and the availability for marriage of Gigi. The resulting publicity boosted sales for both the play and film.

When the movie finally did open, audiences and critics embraced it. Audrey's performance was praised as captivating and authentic. Viewers felt as if she *were* Princess Ann, from the moment she escaped from her confining royal existence to the point at which she was discovered dancing on a barge with the man with whom she had fallen in love and was forced to return to her life of sheltered misery. People fell in love with Audrey's boyish look and soft voice that rose in pitch as her excitement grew. Her long hair had been shorn into the pixie cut that became her trademark. "Paramount's new star," wrote one reviewer, "sparkles and glows with the fire of a finely cut diamond."[2] Another chirped, "Through some private magic, Audrey Hepburn raises the enterprise to the level of high comedy."[3]

The film itself, which has been declared by some to be the greatest romantic comedy ever, received acclaim as the first movie of that genre featuring a sad conclusion. Those who anticipated the journalist to sweep

Princess Ann away were taken aback by what proved to be a memorable ending.

A memorable beginning—that of Audrey's relationship with a new beau—was launched in July 1953 in London, where she returned for the premiere of *Roman Holiday* in England. She attended a party hosted by Ella, at which she was introduced to accomplished American actor Mel Ferrer, a close friend of Gregory Peck, who decided to play matchmaker. Ferrer had been divorced twice and was still wed to Frances Pilchard, who had been his first wife and had remarried him in 1942. He had four kids and was 12 years older than Audrey, but Peck wanted to bring the two together. Ferrer, who was also a stage and film director, was impressed with her unpretentious and gentle yet lively manner. She swooned when he gazed at her with his penetrating eyes. The mutual attraction was immediate and intense.

Melchor Gaston Ferrer was born into wealth and privilege in New Jersey in 1917. His father was a highly successful Cuban-American surgeon practicing in New York City, while his mother enjoyed an aristocratic background. They sent their son to the Ivy League school of Princeton for two years, after which he dabbled in acting, worked as an editor of a small New England newspaper, and wrote a children's book titled *Tito's Hats* that focused on a positive relationship between a father and his son. He was stricken with polio during World War II but recovered and toiled as a disk jockey in Texas and Arkansas before returning to New York in search of theatrical jobs. He finally found success as the director of *Cyrano de Bergerac* on Broadway. Ferrer soon made his way to Hollywood, where he helped establish an acting company located at the La Jolla Playhouse near San Diego, alongside such luminaries as Peck and Joseph Cotton. He remained torn between directing and acting and couldn't find tremendous success in either endeavor.

He did appear in the movie *Lili* in 1953, which Audrey attended and thoroughly enjoyed. She praised his work in the film on their introduction. Ferrer suggested they find a French play more poetic than *Gigi* and star in it together, to which she agreed. He was soon demanding a second divorce from Frances Pilchard, which was awarded without challenge. Ferrer had found his true love and would support Audrey's professional ambitions without question. The couple remained together physically and emotionally all the way to the altar. "It was fascinating to watch Mel move in on Audrey," recalled Hollywood journalist Radie Harris, who had followed Ferrer's career since 1936. "After that first meeting [with Audrey], Mel never let go, and they were inseparable."[4]

Thrilled at the public and critical acclaim Audrey received for her performance in *Roman Holiday*, Paramount quickly searched for another role for her. By the time Audrey met her future husband, she was working on that follow-up, a modern fairy tale titled *Sabrina,* an adaptation of the Samuel Taylor Broadway play, *Sabrina Fair.* The feeling was mutual—Audrey had read the script, seen the Broadway play, and actually requested that Paramount place her in the lead role, that of the daughter of a chauffeur working for a wealthy Long Island family. Sabrina falls for one of the sons, David, who barely knows she exists. Meanwhile, her father scrapes up enough money to send her to finishing school in Paris, where she becomes sophisticated and worldly. She returns to find that David (played by Humphrey Bogart) has taken an interest in her, but his younger brother Linus (portrayed by established star William Holden), who has financially driven ulterior motives, attempts to charm Sabrina away from David.

Audrey had just finished *Gigi,* which opened to packed houses in San Francisco, when she began filming *Sabrina,* for which she was paid the comparatively paltry sum of $15,000. She rented a modest apartment on Long Island for $120 a week and had the local music store often deliver new records, which were awaiting her when she returned from the set. Audrey had become rather domestic—she would listen to such classical greats as Beethoven and Brahms, or jazz legends such as Benny Goodman, while preparing her dinner. She needed the relaxation, for both her personal and professional lives were about to become rather complex. It became apparent from the moment she met Holden that Ferrer would prove not to be the only man in her life. It also became apparent that the legendary Bogart not only didn't get along with Holden, but would be resentful of Audrey, and make no secret of it.

The 35-year-old Holden was at the peak of his career, having won an Academy Award for his performance in *Stalag 17.* He was also married, with two sons and a daughter. Though he remained wed into the 1970s, he had earned a reputation as a notorious hard-drinking womanizer, who even brought other women home to meet his wife, actress Brenda Marshall. He would later claim Audrey had been "the love of [his] life."[5]

"Sometimes at night, I'd get a portable record player and drive out to the country to a little clearing we found," Holden recalled. "We'd put on ballet music . . . Audrey would dance for me in the moonlight. Some of our most magic moments were there."[6]

The affair, however, was fleeting. Though Audrey fell in love with Holden before she began a serious relationship with Ferrer, the circumstances were far from ideal. Holden promised to divorce Brenda to marry her, but he had kept his 1947 vasectomy a secret from Audrey, who told him that she wanted to have children. He eventually told her of the vasectomy, which at once ended the relationship. After the shooting for

*Sabrina* concluded, he responded to the rejection by traveling around the world with the intention of having sex with at least one woman in each country he visited.

Bogart presented a different problem for Audrey as well as for Holden and director Billy Wilder, toward all of whom he expressed anger and scorn. Bogart accepted the role in *Sabrina* after Cary Grant had turned it down, and being considered a second choice was a blow to the ego of arguably the biggest star in Hollywood. Bogart was unfamiliar with roles in romantic comedies, and moreover, he resented that he was forced to play the stuffy older brother, while Holden received all the romantic parts in the film. He considered Holden's popularity a result more of style than substance. The aging Bogart also bitterly complained when Audrey stumbled over a line and caused great consternation on the set when he called Wilder "a Nazi son of a bitch."[7] Wilder was, in fact, an Austrian Jew who had lost his mother, stepfather, and several relatives to the Auschwitz gas chambers during World War II.

Though her affections for Holden had become quite well known, Audrey's persona remained one of innocence and purity. Wilder quickly quashed the possibility of Sabrina making love to the brother played by Bogart, but Audrey proved flirtatious and sexy enough in her role to cause a fistfight between the two brothers. In fact, it is believed that the realism of that brawl between the two main male characters in the movie stemmed from the actual hatred Bogart and Holden held for one another. But Audrey had certainly pulled off her portrayal of a temptress with both moral and romantic motivations.

She was now an established movie star, but there was far less certainty in her personal life. Enter Mel Ferrer, whom she had told in London that she would be interested in working with on stage if he could find a suitable play. At the end of 1953, following the filming of *Sabrina*, he arrived unannounced at her Beverly Hills apartment with two very intriguing bits of information—he had discovered an ideal play with a fairy-tale story line called *Ondine*, and he had gotten divorced. Soon he would be her partner on stage and play and cement a relationship that would result in marriage.

*Ondine* was written by Frenchman Jean Giraudoux and had been quite successful when performed in Paris in 1939. It was based on the medieval legend of a water nymph who wanders away from her home in search of the love of a mortal and falls in love with a gallant knight with mutual feelings. But in the end, the knight betrays her and eventually dies, while she returns to her aquatic sanctuary. Audrey quickly accepted the role of Ondine alongside Ferrer, who would play the knight. A clause in her Paramount contract stipulated that she could act in stage productions that lasted for less than six months, so there were no legal restrictions. The studio also promised a film production of *Ondine* if it proved to be a hit. Playwrights Company paid her $2,500 a week for the play, which represented an increase of 500 percent over her earnings for starring in *Gigi*.

Audrey moved back to New York and rented a Greenwich Village apartment, where she became absorbed in her new role, particularly her wardrobe, which she considered vitally important in establishing herself as an attractive and believable water nymph. Though her role had its light, whimsical moments, it was more dramatic and serious than those she played in *Roman Holiday* and *Gigi*. She was intrigued and excited at the notion of growing professionally, not to mention romantically— Ferrer soon moved in with her. His immediate influence on her personally and on her career became open to speculation. Valentina, who spent a great deal of time with Audrey on the set as a costume designer for *Ondine*, criticized the young actor's new beau for a perceived dominance on the set. Valentina told husband George Schlee that Audrey refused to make even the tiniest alterations on wardrobe without Ferrer's permission. Schlee then took the criticism one step further. "[Ferrer was a] veritable Svengali, exercising influence in every area of Audrey's life, from the food she ate [or didn't eat] to the number of sentences she spoke to reporters," Schlee told *Hollywood Reporter* columnist Radie Harris. "It was as if he couldn't get a handle on his own life or career, so he decided to fixate on Audrey's."[8]

Audrey, however, did feel strongly about her own ideas. When director Alfred Lunt insisted that she dye her naturally chestnut hair blonde for the role of the water nymph, she initially refused. The debate continued right up until opening night in Boston, which kicked off the pre-Broadway run. Audrey finally relented and agreed to bleach her hair blonde, but she regretted it after one glance in the mirror. She then placed on her head a champagne-colored wig that Lunt had prepared for her, but she was again dissatisfied, claiming that her hair looked dead. So she removed the wig and sprinkled gold dust on her own hair, which gave it a fitting magical glow.

What certainly buoyed Audrey's spirits before the Boston performance was a phone call from Lew Wasserman, her Hollywood agent, who informed her that *Sabrina* was receiving tremendous critical success. And the same held true following opening night for *Ondine*. Though the play itself received little praise, her performance was again acclaimed. "Everyone knows that Miss Hepburn is an exquisite young lady, and no one has ever doubted her talent for acting," wrote *New York Times* reviewer

Brooks Atkinson. "But the part of Ondine is a complicated one. It is com-
pounded of intangibles—of moods and impressions, mischief and tragedy.
Somehow Miss Hepburn is able to translate them into the language of the
theater without artfulness or precociousness. She gives a pulsing performance that is all grace and enchantment, disciplined by an instinct for
the realities of the stage."[9]

Audrey was soon awash with more good news. She learned what critics and nearly everyone in the film industry had already suspected—that
she had been nominated for an Academy Award for Best Actress for her
performance in *Roman Holiday*. Even celebrated actor Ingrid Bergman re-
vealed that she was so touched by Audrey's effort in that film that she left
the theater in tears. Audrey could scarcely believe it when she was then
nominated for a Tony Award for *Ondine* so soon after the play had begun
its run.

On March 25, 1954, a mere six weeks after *Ondine* had hit Broadway,
she attended the Academy Awards, which was being held in Hollywood,
but accommodated those on the East Coast with a link-up to the Center
Theater in New York. And when fellow actor Fredric March read the words
that seemed inevitable to everyone but Audrey, "The winner is...Audrey
Hepburn," she was stunned. To a rousing ovation, she raced up the aisle
toward the stage, then turned in the wrong direction and ended up in the
wings. The audience laughed affectionately as she reappeared with a self-
deprecating look on her face and waved to the crowd. She bolted onto the
stage, nearly ran into March as she grabbed the award, gave quick thanks,
and raced off. It was a natural show of pure, unpretentious Audrey, and
those in attendance lapped up every second of it.

Audrey's fluster was real. In fact, she discovered en route to the post
awards press conference that she had lost her Oscar. She was handed another one with which to pose during a photo session before she scrambled
around in a harried search for her Oscar, which she finally found in the ladies' room. Now thoroughly skittish, she returned home and attempted in
vain to fall asleep. The excitement she felt that evening was heightened
just days later at the Tony Awards ceremony, when she learned that she
had won that honor as well. Her acceptance of that award, remarkably,
went off without a hitch. Audrey had become an overnight sensation and
one of the biggest stars in the world. But the spotlight and hectic schedule
had drained her. And her relationship with Ferrer was about to bring her
headaches.

Those headaches didn't come from Ferrer directly, but from those who
criticized her for her habit of awaiting his arrival before facing the ap-
plauding audiences during curtain calls following performances of *Ondine*.

The couple would either jog up to the front of the stage holding hands, or Audrey would turn her head to the crowd until Ferrer met her so they could take their bows together. It has been speculated that Ferrer insisted on joining Hepburn for curtain calls. Lunt, however, put a stop to it, and eventually Audrey accepted the rousing cheers of the audience alone. The director, meanwhile, wrote in a private letter to production supervisor Robert Sherwood that the relationship between Hepburn and Ferrer made the play a "f***ing failure."[10]

One particular critic implored Hepburn to manage her career intelligently and passionately and forget film acting. In a unique column titled "Open Letter to Audrey Hepburn" in *The Nation*, Harold Clurman offered that she performed in *Ondine*

> as if everybody were asking for your telephone number.... [You are] a wonderful instrument with a soul of your own. But, said old Grandpa Ibsen, talent is not just a possession, it is a responsibility. You are at the beginning of your career; because this beginning is so dazzling you must not allow the beginning to become the end. You do not yet know how to transform the outward aspects of a characterization into an inner characterization. You can learn to be a real actress if you do not let the racket, the publicity, the adulation rattle you away from yourself. Keep on acting, studying, working.... Play parts that are risky, parts that are difficult, and do not be afraid to fail! Above all, play on the stage.... Do not trust those who tell you that screen and stage acting are the same species or of equal artistic value.[11]

Sudden stardom didn't bring unbridled joy to Hepburn's life. In fact, the pressure of maintaining or even exceeding the professional standards she had set made her nervous and sometimes downright depressed. Every performance was expected to match that of *Roman Holiday* in artistic greatness and commercial success. She was just 24 years old but dealing with expectations generally heaped on those who had been in the entertainment business for two decades or longer. Her smoking increased from two to three packs a day, and friends noticed on the set of *Ondine* that she had become pale and visibly shaken. She developed asthma. The Playwrights Company doctor offered that she might be on the verge of a complete physical and emotional breakdown. Despite the words of advice from Harold Clurman to concentrate solely on stage acting, she told colleagues that she might very well never perform in another play. And she never did.

The pressure wasn't limited to her career. By the time *Ondine* closed in early July 1954, Ferrer was pressing Hepburn to be his bride. The media picked up on the proposal for marriage, but she continued to hesitate. Hepburn simply did not feel ready for a lifetime commitment. But though she had discarded James Hanson for his insistence that she walk down the aisle with him, she was not about to surrender her relationship with Ferrer.

What she required at the time was rest. And she received it in the form of a vacation in Switzerland. She stayed for a few days in Gstaad, but she found herself being the object of curiosity, just as the princess she portrayed had been in *Roman Holiday*. In fact, she was greeted in the town by hundreds of fans as well as reporters and photographers, who had been informed of her plans. She remained a prisoner in her hotel room before speaking with Ferrer, who arranged for her to stay in a heavily guarded chalet in the Burgenstock, a peaceful Swiss mountain retreat. She agreed to the move, which proved to be a life-altering decision. The quietness and majestic beauty of the Burgenstock, which overlooked Lake Lucerne, provided her the privacy she desperately needed. She instructed the help that only phone calls from her mother and Ferrer were to be put through. She was cared for by a hotel doctor, who prescribed a nourishing and soothing diet and a bedtime of 8:00 P.M. Her blood pressure decreased, and her asthma disappeared. She regained her strength on the tennis court and golf course.

The tranquility allowed Hepburn to reflect clearly on her professional and personal lives. She decided that she indeed wanted to marry Ferrer, who was in Italy shooting a film titled *Madre* (The Mother). She sent him a platinum watch with the inscription "Mad about the man" on his 37th birthday. His production company, aware that a wedding involving he and Audrey Hepburn would result in much needed publicity, allowed Ferrer time off to fly to Switzerland. He offered a proposal that Hepburn accepted despite the objections of her mother, who not only believed a marriage would hinder her daughter's career, but who expressed little respect for her choice of husband.

The couple was wed on September 24, 1954, in a civil ceremony at the home of the mayor of Buochs, Switzerland, on the shores of Lake Lucerne. They repeated their vows the following rainy day in a thirteenth-century Protestant chapel in front of 25 guests, including her reluctant mother. Gregory Peck had been scheduled to serve as best man but was forced to withdraw due to his work schedule. James Hanson turned down his invitation to attend.

And Hepburn, who had exclaimed in an interview during her time with *Ondine* that she would live "in Timbuktu" for the man with whom she fell in love, would make Switzerland her home for the rest of her life. She had grown quite fond of the quaint, peaceful nation that allowed her to recuperate from her emotional and physical distress. "There is no place in the world where I felt so much at peace," Hepburn exclaimed. "It's my very private stomping ground."[12]

The private stomping ground could never prevent intrusions into her private life. But as she and Ferrer set off on their honeymoon, Hepburn felt blissful. And that was quite a welcome and foreign emotion.

## NOTES

1. Barry Paris, *Audrey Hepburn* (New York: G. P. Putnam's Sons, 1996), 81.

2. "Princess Apparent," *Time Magazine*, September 7, 1953, 63.

3. *New Yorker*, August 29, 1953.

4. Radie Harris, *Radie's World: The Memoirs of Radie Harris* (London: W. W. Allen, 1975), 58.

5. Paris, *Audrey Hepburn*, 93.

6. Alexander Walker, *Audrey: Her Real Story* (New York: St. Martin's Griffin, 1994), 90.

7. Donald Spoto, *Enchantment: The Life of Audrey Hepburn* (New York: Harmony Books, 2006), 111.

8. Charles Higham, *Audrey: The Life of Audrey Hepburn* (New York: Macmillan, 1984), 112.

9. Brooks Atkinson, "First Night at the Theatre," *New York Times*, February 19, 1954, 23.

10. Paris, *Audrey Hepburn*, 103.

11. Harold Clurman, "Open Letter to Audrey Hepburn," *The Nation*, March 6, 1954, 206.

12. Paris, *Audrey Hepburn*, 112.

*Audrey as a young girl before the outbreak of World War II. Courtesy of Photofest.*

*The 1951 Broadway play* Gigi *was Hepburn's breakthrough performance. Courtesy of Photofest.*

*Hepburn portraying a lonely princess in* Roman Holiday. *Courtesy of Photofest.*

*Hepburn displays her only Oscar, which she won for* Roman Holiday *in 1954. Courtesy of Photofest.*

*Hepburn with her first husband, Mel Ferrer. Courtesy of Photofest.*

*Hepburn dancing with the great Fred Astaire during the filming of* Funny Face *in 1957. Courtesy of Photofest.*

*Hepburn strikes a pose in a publicity still* for Breakfast at Tiffany's *in 1961. Courtesy of Photofest.*

*Hepburn, as Eliza Doolittle, co-starred with Rex Harrison (right) in the 1964 film* My Fair Lady. *Courtesy of Photofest.*

*Hepburn in one of her most adventurous roles: a terrorized blind woman in the 1967 film* Wait Until Dark. *Courtesy of Photofest.*

*Hepburn volunteering for UNICEF in war-torn Somalia in the early 1980s. Courtesy of Photofest.*

# Chapter 6

# JUGGLING PRIVATE AND PUBLIC LIVES

The newlyweds couldn't wait to be alone. After a brief reception at a private golf club, they pulled a fast one on the media, who were told they were heading straight for Italy. Instead, they spent their wedding night nestling by a roaring fire in her Swiss chalet, where they remained for the next three days. They did fly to Italy on September 28, when Mel returned to work, renting a villa near the seaside resort of Anzio. His invigorated bride did read a few scripts for potential film roles but continued to enjoy her freedom, whiling away the hours in the garden and preparing Italian dishes in the kitchen. And when Mel was away, she wasn't alone. She kept company with the cats, doves, dogs, and donkey that roamed around the grounds.

Hepburn did accept one public appearance, helping to raise money for Dutch war invalids in Amsterdam in early November. She agreed to sign photographs at a nearby department store, but the plan backfired when a group of young fans smashed showcases and violently shoved their way through to catch a glimpse of her. She was forced to hightail it out of the store, vowing that she would agree to no more public appearances unless adequate protection had been guaranteed. Hepburn had been uneasy, and sometimes even frightened, her entire life by the prospect of meeting strangers, and that experience heightened those fears.

As a beautiful young star, however, Hepburn was in the wrong environment for avoiding social situations. And soon she was flung back into the professional world, as many columnists offered their view that Mel had taken control of her life. Such an opinion was not unwarranted. Ever since her father abandoned the family before World War II, she had sought a

strong replacement. Mel boasted a strong personality that some believed
bordered on domineering. Hepburn biographer Charles Higham took it
a step further. "Audrey had become increasingly insecure, and began to
change from a somewhat innocent and jittery girl propelled into enormous fame overnight into an authentically recessive and neurotic personality," he wrote. "She clung to Ferrer in a relationship in which she was
totally dependent on him for every move and every decision. In addition,
the relationship was curiously ironic in that her talent far surpassed that of
her husband, and her sensitivity and delicacy of nature were more refined
than his. But, not without a degree of conscious control, he asserted his
masculine authority by overpowering her completely."[1]

Though such a view can be debated, Audrey unquestionably yearned to
keep her private and public lives separate. She even chastised her grandmother for secretly sending photos of her wedding to the German-language
weekly *Wochenschau*, which published them in a full-page spread. Frau
Foregger was elderly and living on a limited income, so her motivation
was purely financial. But her granddaughter wrote her a terse letter criti-
cizing her for selling photos that had been earmarked only for close family
members. Foregger later apologized, and the two forged a loving relationship thereafter—Hepburn sent her a generous check every Christmas to
help pay the bills.

Hepburn was about to receive quite a gift herself. Soon after the wedding, she became pregnant. Far from considering pregnancy and child
rearing a burden and a hindrance to her career, Hepburn was thrilled. She
would, on many occasions, state her view that giving birth was her most
important achievement in life. Audrey and Mel reveled in each other's
love during the Christmas holidays in 1954, exchanging matching blue and
yellow cashmere sweaters and having another one knitted for the baby.

While their love blossomed, some of the bloom began to fall off the
rose in Hepburn's career. Soon after *Sabrina* was released, it became apparent she would not receive anywhere near the acclaim she had earned
for her breakout performance in *Roman Holiday*. The critical reaction to
her latest film was merely lukewarm and, in some cases, quite negative.
While panning Bogart as a "frail, lisping old man," critic Clayton Cole
of the British magazine *Film and Filming* was scathing in his criticism of
Hepburn, writing, "Sabrina is the prick that bursts the fair bubble that was
Audrey Hepburn in *Roman Holiday*. Surely the vogue for asexuality can go
no further than this weird hybrid with butchered hair. Of course none of
this would really matter if her charm and grace were sincere, but I'm afraid
that she is letting her calculation show."[2]

Other reviews were kinder, but it had become apparent that Hepburn
couldn't rest on her laurels. Yet the moviegoing public, perhaps driven

at least to some extent by their curiosity about her follow-up to *Roman Holiday*, stormed the movie theaters in droves. *Sabrina* was on its way to becoming the third highest grossing film of 1954. And she did receive a second Academy Award nomination for her role, losing out in 1955 to Grace Kelly, who won the Oscar for her performance in *The Country Girl*.

Media attacks didn't end with her performance in *Sabrina*. Some journalists claimed Hepburn was only accepting roles from producers who would provide Ferrer with a part as well. She did indeed request her husband as a costar when offered by producers Dinto de Laurentiis and Carlo Ponti the role of Natasha in *War and Peace*, a 6 million dollar epic that had been inspired by the Leo Tolstoy classic. Hepburn knew that she not only had to return to the screen, but that her career required that every role be a starring one in a potential blockbuster. Yet she had never felt more content than in her private moments with her husband. She had come to the realization, even after achieving such tremendous critical and financial success, that her happiness wasn't tied in with professional ambition. And indeed, her career would always be placed far behind her personal relationships on her list of priorities.

"She never had the burning desire to become and remain a movie star, as do most actresses, but instead cared only for personal happiness, peace, love, her children, a husband whom she loved and who loved her," said Henry Rogers, who had become her publicist and close friend. "Although she loved acting, she wanted to work less and spend more time in private."[3]

After Ferrer was given the role of Prince Andrei, Hepburn committed to playing Natasha in *War and Peace* for 350,000 dollars (Mel earned 100,000 dollars for his part). But the production would have to be postponed from late winter 1954 until after she gave birth in July 1955. Her character, after all, was slight of build and quite active during the frantic days of Napoleon's invasion of Russia. The change of plans caused more than a bit of anxiety for the producers, who had gone to great lengths to secure military personnel from Italy and Yugoslavia to play French and Russian troops in the film as well as the creating of thousands of uniforms, all of which had to be individually fitted. Some 8,000 horses and 3,000 cannon also had to be procured. The task was enormous.

The role of Natasha proved quite intriguing for Hepburn, whose own experiences during World War II heightened her appreciation for the experiences of her character. She studied the book *War and Peace* as well as other Tolstoy novels and learned more about the Russian aristocracy of which Natasha was a part.

Hepburn would soon be juggling her professional and personal lives again. She yearned deeply to be accepted by her new stepchildren, including two that visited her in Switzerland during their school vacations. In an attempt to win over their friendship and set herself apart from their real mother, she insisted they call her "Audrey." She understood that Mel's children were going through difficult times in light of their parents' recent divorce.

Determined to make her marriage work, Audrey and Mel attempted to arrange their schedules so they wouldn't remain apart for more than a couple days at a time. She also searched for future roles in movies in which her husband could land a part. Some offer that Hepburn even turned down the role of Joan of Arc because Otto Preminger opted to cast Richard Widmark as Dauphin, rather than Ferrer. The role of Joan of Arc eventually thrust Jean Seberg into at least temporary stardom. The newlyweds instead tried to sell the idea of creating the movie version of *Ondine*, but there were no takers because of doubts that the sensational play could be successfully transformed into an on-screen production.

Late in the winter of 1955, Hepburn returned to Switzerland and was soon eagerly awaiting the birth of her child. She felt at ease in the little country that had protected her sanity a year earlier. She spent a great deal of time at one particular café near Lake Lucerne, in which she became quite close to the proprietor and staff. Hepburn cherished the serenity of the area and the closeness of the people. The love she received from the locals seemed far more genuine than the praise she received from the hand shakers and well-wishers in show business, who simply looked to ride her coattails. The modern world appeared to her so pleasantly distant in this Swiss village, where doctors still made house calls and the concerns about her pregnancy felt real.

The justification of such concerns was realized in March when, to her horror, Hepburn's pregnancy was terminated. One day she was feeling pain and uneasiness, and the next day she learned that she had suffered a miscarriage.

"I wanted to cancel the movie," Hepburn said. "I wanted to cancel my life. But I moved forward for Mel. He thought that *War and Peace* would help me get over my grief and I felt it would help him recapture his career. I'm not sure it accomplished either of those goals, but it helped pass a desolate time."[4]

The blow brought the couple closer together and increased Hepburn's emotional dependence on her husband. Her motivation to ease the pain by leaving it behind also helped her immerse herself in her work with increased concentration and passion, both of which were required to successfully portray Natasha, one of history's most complex literary characters and greatest heroines.

The closely cropped hairstyle that helped make Hepburn famous had to be lengthened in deference to the role, which saddened fans and media members, who would have preferred she maintained her adolescent look for at least a bit longer. But, after all, she was closing in on her 25th birthday, though Natasha was only 15 years old. Hepburn was to portray a lively girl who was no longer a child, but not yet a young woman. It was a difficult role for a worldly type who had lived through so much. Hepburn was no longer the wide-eyed girl she was to play.

Meanwhile, she and Mel searched out roles that allowed them to work together, or at least simultaneously in the same city. Before Hepburn even began work on *War and Peace*, she accepted a role in a comedy titled *Love in the Afternoon*, which would be directed by Billy Wilder and costar Maurice Chevalier and heartthrob Gary Cooper. But she didn't agree to it until it had been confirmed that Mel had landed a part in *Elena et les homes*, another comedy that would be shot in Paris at the same time.

One film adaptation she refused for quite different reasons was *The Diary of Anne Frank*, for which many believed she would have been ideal. The story of a Jewish girl who spent World War II hiding with her family in a secret annex in Amsterdam before they were discovered and sent to the Auschwitz concentration camp simply hit too close to home for Hepburn. She had begun reading the book in 1946 and was quite moved, but she couldn't be convinced to take on the lead role. "I read it, and it destroyed me," she said. "I was not reading it as a book, as printed pages. This was my life....I've never been the same again, it affected me so deeply."[5] It would be emotionally taxing enough to play the role of a girl in the midst of war in the early nineteenth century, let alone one who experienced the same horrors in the same war that Audrey had a decade past.

Paramount was looking to capture the essence of the book and transform it into a film epic, which might explain the nearly four-hour length of the movie. Such a monumental goal was commonplace in the mid-1950s for filmmakers, who were at wit's end trying to lure back to the theater folks who now spent most of their evenings lounging on their couches watching television. *War and Peace* director King Vidor periodically reminded his cast that among their obligations was drawing the public away from their TV sets.

The filming was targeted for 12 weeks but ran from July through November. Hepburn was forced to wear heavy gowns and furs as she tromped around the artificial snow in the unbearable heat of the Italian summer. She was exhausted by the end of her 10-hour workdays. But though still distressed over the loss of her child and leery about the complexity of the film as well as the dominance of the battle scenes over the human

element, Hepburn emerged with critical acclaim, while American costar
Henry Fonda was panned as not believable for his efforts as hero Pierre
Bezhukov.

In the end, however, *War and Peace* proved too grandiose for its own
good. The battles between the Russian and French soldiers were quite exciting and realistic, but many critics claimed that the personal moments
shared by the characters were overwhelmed by the scope of the film itself, which was shot in Technicolor and seen on the wide screen. The
characters themselves were drowned out. It didn't go unnoticed by the
media. One critic claimed the film was "oddly mechanical and emotionally sterile [and] the characters seem second-rate people, hackneyed and
without much depth.... The human stories are sketchy and inconsequen-
tial."[6] But Hepburn was generally praised for her performance.

What some critics did claim was that her husband was controlling her
career. One magazine writer charged that her relationship with Mel was
"a kind of master-to-slave one, with Mel directing her life, using her career as a stepping stone for his own."[7] But Hepburn vehemently defended
herself:

> How can people say Mel makes all my decisions, that he de-
> cides what I am going to play, and with whom, and where!
> I know how scrupulously correct he is, and how he loathes to
> give an opinion unless I ask for it. This is *because* we want so
> badly to keep our careers separate. We don't *want* to interfere
> with each other....
>
> I've been fending for myself since I was thirteen and think-
> ing very carefully about a lot of important problems, and I don't
> think I've made many bad decisions. I'm very proud of that,
> about my ability to think for myself, and no one, not even my
> husband, whom I adore, can persuade me to do something
> against my own judgment.[8]

Hepburn's desire to remain close to her husband was sometimes misread
as dependence on him in all areas of her life. She grew indignant when it
was claimed that Mel was cast for his role in *War and Peace* only because
she insisted on it, offering that her husband had been considered ideal
for the part of Prince Andrei before the couple had even been married.
But the criticism continued from those who believed Mel to be self-
serving, manipulative, and even jealous of his wife's talent and success.

The offers, however, continued to pour in. In the fall of 1955, Hepburn
met with legendary writer Tennessee Williams and producer Hal Wallis,

who offered her the role of a spinster teacher in the film version of *Summer and Smoke*, but she turned it down because, according to Wallis, her request that she costar with her husband was rejected. She declined dozens of possibilities from Associated British and also an offer from Paramount to play the *son* of Napoleon in *L'Aiglon*. That radical idea was nixed; in fact, the movie was never made. Instead, Hepburn lost an opportunity to play the title role in *Jane Ayre* because the male lead considered her too attractive for the role. Instead, she accepted the part of clerk-turned-model Jo Stockton in *Funny Face*.

Hepburn couldn't have asked for a more diversionary film and one with a greater contrary spirit to the gripping and dour *War and Peace*. In *Funny Face*, she would be dancing and singing on the River Seine with the legendary Fred Astaire, with whom she had dreamed of working, despite the fact that he was 37 years her senior. The role was originally earmarked for little-known actress Carol Haney, but the hope of attracting a bigger name motivated MGM to send the script to Hepburn, though the studio believed it would be considered small potatoes to the young star. Paramount refused to lend Hepburn to MGM, deciding instead to produce the movie itself.

Hepburn, however, yearned for a lighter project as a follow-up to the grueling *War and Peace*. She devoured the script in about two hours—speed reading indeed, considering it generally took her three weeks to soak in every word of a potential role—after which she joyfully burst into the room in which Mel was working and told him enthusiastically that this was the part she'd been longing for. Her acceptance turned a possible red light for the movie a bright green. And she took the part for a mere 150,000 dollars.

Audrey and Mel managed to remain together throughout the shooting of the film, which began with three months in Hollywood, followed by a month in Paris, where such landmarks as the Eiffel Tower, the Louvre, and the Arc de Triomphe were in full display in the film.

Among her many diversions in Paris were jazz clubs. Mel had turned her on to the musical genre, for which she had developed a fanaticism. The couple not only carried a portable phonograph and records with them from one location to the next, but they frequented the many jazz clubs in the French capital. Her passion for jazz also heightened her overall appreciation of music and put her even more in the mood to work with Astaire, in what promised to be the most ballyhooed musical of the year. Hepburn was terrified at the prospect of going step for step with Astaire, but her enthusiasm for the role motivated her to throw every bit of energy and concentration into her dancing.

"I never saw anyone work so hard," recalled screenwriter Leonard Ger-she 40 years later. "She was tireless in learning both the songs and the dances. It wasn't like Cyd Charisse or Ginger Rogers, who did it all the time. [Producer/arranger] Roger Edens would say, 'Audrey, take tomorrow off. You've been working sixteen hours a day.' She'd say, 'No, I'll be here at nine.' And then she'd be there at eight."[9]

One can't blame Hepburn for her desire to work with Astaire. But the feeling was mutual. Astaire informed her at a party that he had dreamed of working with her, which caused both of them to break out in laughter. It was apparent from the start that their personalities meshed and that the costars would get along well.

Audrey and Mel strolled into the plush Paris hotel in which they stayed with 20 cabin trunks awaiting them. The rule that guests would accept the furnishings already in place would certainly not do for Hepburn, who insisted on decorating her room in the same style accentuating the Swiss chalet with which she had grown so much in love. She meticulously marked every package to easily find and place every knickknack where she wanted it in her suite. And she would follow the same routine in every work residence in which she lived throughout her career.

All that prevented an ideal experience for Hepburn in *Funny Face* was Mother Nature. The spring weather in Paris was unseasonably cold and rainy in 1956, which caused scenes that were intended to be soaked in sunshine to be delayed. She often left her hotel for a full day's work, only to return disappointed a couple hours later because the chilly, damp con-ditions prevented shooting. The schedule fell hopelessly behind. In one scene, she and Astaire were to dance across a lawn, through a walled garden, across a bridge, and into a wooden raft as the sun shone brightly. Instead, they slipped and slid in the mud time and again, causing a long holdup, though the friendship that had been forged between the two al-lowed them to turn their frustration into laughter.

The opportunity to work with Astaire would remain a cherished memory for the rest of her life. As she presented him with a Lifetime Achievement Award by the American Film Institute 25 years later, Hep-burn spoke of her feelings for the debonair actor and dancer and recalled fondly the experience of having the honor of being his partner. "I could feel myself turn into solid lead while my heart sank into my own two left feet," she recalled. "Then, suddenly, I felt a hand around my waist, and with his inimitable grace and lightness, Fred literally swept me off my feet. I experienced the thrill that all women at some point in their lives have dreamed of—to dance just once with Fred Astaire."[10]

Hepburn was particularly proud that her singing was deemed strong enough that the producers dropped the notion of dubbing over her voice. Meanwhile, her insecurities melted away as she worked with Astaire.

And so did her weight. Her notoriously birdlike appetite shrunk to virtually nothing during the hot summer months, causing her to lose 17 pounds and drop to a painfully light 92. Her mother flew in from London, attempting to come to the rescue with chocolate bars, which Audrey had never been able to resist. But, alas, her daughter with a notorious sweet tooth actually turned them down.

The waiflike figure certainly wasn't hampering Hepburn's career. But a rather curious strain in her career had emerged; that is, she was consistently paired up with actors far older than she. Bogart, Fonda, Astaire, and (soon) Gary Cooper were all old enough to be her father. Though she had been placed at times in romantic situations, working with such costars tended to remove any implicit sexuality from the relationship and much of the sensuality from her persona. In addition, despite her beautiful, angelic face, her boyish figure often precluded the strong, lustful feelings that male filmgoers had for voluptuous, curvy stars of the day such as Marilyn Monroe and Brigitte Bardot. That was soon to change.

## NOTES

1. Charles Higham, *Audrey: The Life of Audrey Hepburn* (New York: Macmillan, 1984), 85–86.

2. Clayton Cole, *Film & Filming,* October 1954, 20. Article title unavailable.

3. Donald Spoto, *Enchantment: The Life of Audrey Hepburn* (New York: Harmony Books, 2006), 132.

4. Diana Maychick, *Audrey Hepburn: An Intimate Portrait* (New York: Carol, 1993), 126.

5. Alexander Walker, *Audrey: Her Real Story* (New York: St. Martin's Griffin, 1994), 121.

6. Bosley Crowther, *New York Times*, August 22, 1956, 26. Article title unavailable.

7. Carl Clement, "Look Where You're Going, Audrey," *Photoplay,* June 1957, 84.

8. Mary Worthington Jones, "My Husband Doesn't Run Me," *Photoplay,* April 1956, 105.

9. Barry Paris, *Audrey Hepburn* (New York: G. P. Putnam's Sons, 1996), 127–28.

10. Walker, *Audrey*, 130.

# Chapter 7

# FINALLY A MOM

Just weeks after Hepburn completed *Funny Face* in July 1956, she began toiling immediately on a far more sexually explicit film titled *Love in the Afternoon*, which was being directed by Billy Wilder, with whom she worked in *Sabrina*. Malnourished and, as usual, lacking confidence, she feared that she wouldn't be appreciated by costar Gary Cooper. And her husband was concerned that she might fall for the handsome, hunky actor, just as she did for William Holden years earlier.

"I kept having this premonition that Gary Cooper, whom I had always admired, was going to turn out to hate me like Humphrey Bogart," Hepburn said. "I was working myself into a frenzy. Mel wasn't much help because, frankly, he was incensed that I was even thinking of the time when I met Bill Holden. Mel was a jealous husband, and I always loved that about him."[1]

The strapping Cooper had been the darling of the American cinema and female movie patrons for three decades, but he was 55 years old. In fact, he gained the role of Flannagan, the aging American businessman and incorrigible womanizer, only after heartthrob Cary Grant had turned it down. Hepburn was to assume the role of Arianne, a music student and daughter of a private detective played by French star Maurice Chevalier. Arianne is initially intrigued by Flannagan's philandering but soon falls in love with him, and in an effort to convince him of her own worldliness, she concocts stories about her love affairs with other men. She eventually wins him over in the final scene, when he is about to leave her at a train station in Paris, but instead sweeps her into his arms.

As had become typical, Hepburn entered the production with tremendous uncertainty that quickly dissipated. In fact, she enjoyed working on *Love in the Afternoon* as much as she had any previous project. The cast and crew would not go their separate ways after hard days of filming; rather, they reveled in each other's company at a nearby club, where they talked, laughed, and drank martinis well into the night.

Cooper spoke glowingly of Hepburn, praising her for her enthusiasm and energy. Like his character and despite his marriage, Cooper was a notorious ladies' man, but there would be no romantic interludes with his young costar. Hepburn instead awaited the arrival of her husband, who was away for long intervals in the south of France filming *The Vintage*. But for the first time since her wedding, she felt strong enough emotionally to run her life without pining for Mel.

What she did pine for in regard to the man in her life was a chance to work alongside him in a film version of *My Fair Lady*. Before beginning work on *Love in the Afternoon*, she flew to New York to see friend Cathleen Nesbitt perform in the stage musical, which starred Rex Harrison and Julie Andrews. Hepburn yearned for the role of a cockney ragamuffin who is taught worldly ways by a snobbish professor, who would, of course, be played by Ferrer.

That would have to wait, however. In fact, so would her career. After finishing two films in one year and despite her enormous popularity, Hepburn announced her plans to take 1957 off. She embraced the role of housewife, turning down several movie offers in the process. Instead of acting, she returned to Burgenstock, where she planted flowers in her garden, cooked for her husband, puttered around the home, and enjoyed a well-deserved and much desired rest.

It was during this period that Mel discovered through intensive research that Audrey's father was still alive. Her mother had told her years earlier that he had passed away, but Mel was suspicious and decided to try to track him down. And indeed, he found evidence that Joseph was living near Dublin. She flew to Ireland to meet him, but the reunion turned out to be a tremendous disappointment. He seemed quite aloof and disinterested in his daughter. He had married a woman 30 years younger. The awkward meeting ended abruptly. Audrey would rarely see her father again, though she did send him monthly checks, until he passed away in his nineties.

Soon she was off to Mexico, where Mel was on location, having taken a supporting role in the film adaptation of the Hemingway classic *The Sun Also Rises*. She felt thoroughly relaxed as nothing more than wife, speaking later about how she adored her time spent at home while her husband worked. But her sabbatical was short-lived. Mel talked her into joining him in a 90-minute American made-for-TV movie titled *Mayerling* about the doomed relationship between Austrian crown prince Rudolph and his mistress Mary Vetsera in the late nineteenth century. Hepburn was paid 157,000 dollars for her efforts, then a record for a performer in a television drama. But as time lapsed during the production, it became painfully obvious that while Audrey's stock was on the rise, that of her husband was rapidly declining. Mel simply no longer warranted a leading role. Though a married couple, the on-screen chemistry between them lacked credibility, and the critics lambasted his performance.

Audrey, on the other hand, received praise for her dancing, singing, and overall work in *Funny Face* as *Love in the Afternoon* was being prepared for release. It was ironic, however, that a woman acclaimed for her talent felt most comfortable and content playing the role of housewife, while Mel couldn't earn the plaudits for his work that he so desperately desired. Yet though she managed to reject what appeared to be appropriate roles for a short time, her vow to stay away from films for a year was broken when, in January 1957, she accepted the lead role in *The Nun's Story*. Her fee was 200,000 dollars, a rather paltry sum in comparison to the money she earned in previous films. But the contract also stipulated that she would receive 10 percent of the gross box office receipts—and the film earned several times more than the $3.5 million it cost to make.

Though the film is fictional, it is based on the true experiences of a Belgian nun named Sister Luke who renounces her vows after 17 years of toiling as a missionary in the Congo, which, at the time, was under Belgian rule. She leaves the African nation to join the Belgian resistance during World War II and finds her spirituality challenged by the conflict.

Though it is widely assumed that Hepburn accepted the part because of its parallels to her own experiences in Belgium during World War II, it must be remembered that she turned down the lead role in *The Diary of Anne Frank* for the same reason. What attracted her to *The Nun's Story* was the opportunity to pay tribute to Marie-Louise Habets, the real-life Sister Luke, who had become a civilian nurse and had worked with the United Nations Rehabilitation and Relief Administration to help displaced persons in postwar Germany. The movie focused entirely on her life; in fact, all the World War II scenes were eventually removed.

In late January 1958, she accompanied Fred Zinneman, who had directed such classics as *From Here to Eternity, High Noon,* and *Oklahoma!,* and the rest of the crew to the Belgian Congo for the first two months of shooting. The group would encounter a snake or two under the breakfast table and temperatures that soared to as high as 130 degrees, but overall, they were quite comfortable. Hepburn even discovered that wearing a nun's habit actually sealed her from the heat.

The filming continued in Rome, and when completed, the uncut version was shown to Habets, who was taken aback by its stark reality. She was even moved by the religious aspect of it, despite the fact that she had left the convent years earlier.

"It was too overwhelming," Habets said. "I'm never going to see it again because if I do I'm going to run right back to the convent.... I could just sit there and cry my eyes out, not with regret, but because of the beauty of it."[2]

Though not as popular as some of her other films, *The Nun's Story* brought Hepburn more critical acclaim than any movie in which she had starred since *Roman Holiday*. Some believed it was an even better performance because of its complexities. The serious nature of the film, which some believed should have been produced in a documentary format, changed the perception of her by movie fans and those in the industry. She proved that she could thrive as an actor in more artful, thought-provoking roles. Some had considered her attraction more style than substance. After her performance in *The Nun's Story,* she began to be taken more seriously as an actor.

*Films in Review* critic Henry Hart was one of many who praised Hepburn and offered hope that her portrayal of Sister Luke would "forever silence those who have thought her less an actress than a symbol of the sophisticated child-woman. In *The Nun's Story,* Miss Hepburn reveals the kind of acting talent that can project inner feelings of both depth and complexity so skillfully you must scrutinize her intently on a second and third viewing to perceive how she does it."[3]

Hepburn worked on *The Nun's Story* from January through June in both the Congo and Italy. But there was no rest for the weary. She had promised her husband that she would star in a film he was directing for MGM titled *Green Mansions* about a teenage girl named Rima in the South American rain forest that falls in love with Abel, a political refugee, and is eventually murdered by a group of savage jungle dwellers. The film, which was based on a popular 1904 novel by W. H. Hudson, required a young leading man, which turned out to be 26-year-old Anthony Perkins, who later found fame as a demented killer in the Alfred Hitchcock thriller *Psycho*.

The movie was doomed from the start. Rather than film on location in the South American rain forest, or even in suitable areas of Mexico or Florida, MGM opted to shoot in its own studios in Culver City, California. It was not only the only time Mel directed his wife, but it would prove to be an unmitigated flop. And to make matters worse for Hepburn, who had yet to be buoyed by the critical praise of the still unreleased *The Nun's Story*, she experienced a car accident in mid-July that resulted in back and neck injuries. She crashed into a car that was swerving toward her, but the driver of that vehicle sued her for damages. The case was eventually dismissed, but Hepburn maintained her vow that she would never again drive a car.

The film was quickly released and universally panned. It received little public attention, but, fortunately for Hepburn, *The Nun's Story* was released three months later. At the time, it was the highest-grossing film in Warner Bros. history. Fans wrapped around the Rockefeller Center and waited for five hours to purchase tickets. The movie opened nationally in July. It came as no surprise when three weeks after the film premiered, she was nominated for her third Academy Award for her performance. Though she lost to Simone Signoret, who portrayed an aging woman in love with a younger man in *Room at the Top*, Hepburn did receive the New York Film Critics' Award for 1959.

Soon she received a script for a classic western, an immensely popular genre at which she had been anxious to try her talents. In *The Unforgiven*, she would play the role of Rachel Zachary, a Kiowa Indian girl and sister of a chief, living with a white family in the Texas panhandle in the 1860s. She felt uneasy about one scene in which she was to ride a horse, greatly because she had been thrown off a pony and broken her collarbone as a young child. But she embarked on riding lessons to alleviate the fear. It was, after all, a project for which she yearned. She wasn't about to reject it based on an unpleasant experience more than 20 years earlier. Costars such as legendary Lillian Gish and the well-established Burt Lancaster also piqued her interest.

More good news followed from Burgenstock, where she helped Mel recover emotionally from the failure of *Green Mansions*. At about the same time she was signing the contract for *The Unforgiven*, she learned that she was pregnant again. The couple celebrated, but tragedy was once again on the horizon.

The newest project gave Hepburn the opportunity to work with noted director John Huston, who had earned a reputation for his brilliance with westerns. His informality and engaging personality helped her relax and gave her confidence that she would perform well in such a genre. The entire film was to be shot in the Durango region of Mexico, a more primitive location than in Texas, which had been deemed far too modernized.

Despite her lessons, Hepburn remained frightened over the prospect of riding a horse. She even lied to Huston, claiming to him that she had no experience with it. He offered the use of a stunt double but added that she would be needed to ride for about 50 yards and that she would be given every bit of protection that could be mustered. Huston even provided her with an experienced instructor and tried to assure her that she would be safe.

The horse, named Diablo, had other ideas. It appeared tame enough for Hepburn to attempt to canter it over a rather narrow point by a river-bank, but perhaps due to a combination of uneasiness with a new rider, discomfort by her sitting sidesaddle in a long skirt, and the bright lights in its eyes, the stallion bucked. Hepburn was thrown off and slammed hard onto the ground, where she writhed in pain, convinced that she had broken her back. She was placed gingerly onto a stretcher and taken by plane to a Durango hospital, where Mel had rushed to her side. As X-rays revealed several broken vertebrae and Hepburn fretted about the fetus, *The Unforgiven* was put on hold for three weeks.

Doctors gave her hope that the child would survive the accident. Mean-while, Hepburn was placed in a protective and quite uncomfortable ortho-pedic brace so she could continue filming, though her husband attempted to convince her to drop the project. He even attempted to express to Huston his feeling that the movie should have been cancelled altogether, much to the irritation of the legendary director. Not only did Huston dis-miss the idea, he forced Hepburn to mount the horse again—brace and all—though for that occasion, Diablo had been sedated. This time the scene went off without a hitch, despite her fears.

It didn't matter. It is widely believed that Hepburn was miscast as an Indian girl who is raised by a frontier family, and the film was far from a critical or financial success. Even Huston panned it. "Some of my pictures I don't care for, but *The Unforgiven* is the only one I actually dislike," he said years later. "I watched it on television one night recently, and after about half a reel I had to turn the damned thing off. I couldn't bear it."[4]

Hepburn couldn't bear her child. She had returned to Burgenstock for the duration of her term but suffered another miscarriage. She became overwhelmed with resentment. She blamed Huston for forcing her to ride a horse and herself for giving in to his demand. She felt destined to never have a child with Mel, despite their intense love for one another. Hepburn fell into a deep depression. Her appetite diminished, and more weight dropped off her already painfully thin body. She fell to 98 pounds and intensified her smoking habit, increasing her consumption to three packs a day. Though all the evidence against smoking had yet to be re-vealed, it was widely believed even at that time that smoking three packs a day was harmful.

Hepburn considered retiring from acting at the tender age of 30, but she knew it was not a realistic possibility. Mel planned a six-city tour to coincide with the release of *The Nun's Story* in Europe to take her mind off the miscarriage and the resulting anger. But this was no vacation. Though she was honored in Doorn, where a street was renamed "Audrey Hepburn-laan," she was besieged through the continent by fans and reporters who peppered her with questions she was in no mood to answer.

Though she had yet to find consistency in her career, she was still a critically acclaimed star. She had every reason to be content professionally, but this did not translate into personal happiness in Hepburn's case. Her overriding goal in life was to be a mother despite, and perhaps as a result of, her own miserable childhood experiences, which included her parents' divorce and the abandonment of the family by her father. But following her second miscarriage, she was justified in her fears that she would never bring a child to term. Though such longings overwhelmed any professional considerations, she knew that only going back to work would allow her to place her misery over her miscarriage in the back of her mind.

Soon, however, she was pregnant again. She was being considered in late 1959 for lead roles in such classics as *Cleopatra* and *West Side Story*, but she vowed that nothing was going to prevent her from giving this pregnancy its best chance to succeed. She nervously knitted baby clothes while fearing the worst. She accompanied Mel to Italy while he filmed *Blood and Roses* and to France as he worked on the *Hands of Orlac*, but otherwise remained close to home. And on January 17, 1960, much to her relief and delight, Sean Ferrer was born.

Four years later, she spoke of the experience and her unbridled joy of fulfilling a lifetime dream. She remembered every detail. "Like all new mothers, I couldn't believe, at first, that he was really for me and that I could keep him....Even when I was little, what I wanted most was to have a child....And I wanted lots of babies....From the time I had Sean, I hung onto my marriage because of him, and more and more, I began to resent the time I spent away from him on location. That was always the real me. The movies were fairy tales."[5]

Hepburn had grandiose plans for her son socially. She expressed a desire to have him meet people from all over the world, soaking in a wide range of cultural diversity. She spoke about Sean doing his part in making the world a better place to live. But soon after his birth, she began to fret about his safety. She even worried about the unlikely occurrence of a kidnapping.

She was torn between her desires to remain home with Sean and return to work, but there was really no choice. Money needed to be made, and after the disaster of *Green Mansions*, it appeared that Mel's career was foundering. Though she did want to spend as much time as possible with her baby, she also sought new adventures in acting. She had already turned down several roles, which had irritated the studio, so she knew it was time to find a worthy project. And that was the part of Holly Golightly in *Breakfast at Tiffany's,* which was written for Marilyn Monroe, who turned it down due to a contractual obligation to Twentieth Century Fox. It would prove to be one of Hepburn's most noteworthy and enduring roles.

The film was based loosely on a Truman Capote novella, which featured a poor young woman who abandons her husband and stepchildren in Texas and travels to New York to seek excitement, and eventually meets the richest man in the world. Attracted only by his money and attempting to sway him to marry her, she turns to promising sexual favors for men, though she never delivers. It was quite a stretch for Hepburn.

Holly then befriends a struggling writer named Paul (played by George Peppard), whose financial hardships are alleviated by a wealthy older woman trying to buy his affections. In the end, Holly and Paul fall in love. Hepburn felt uneasy about playing the role of an extroverted woman since she was quite the opposite. She forced herself through it, however, but questioned her performance during filming.

Among the highlights of the film was Audrey's crooning of "Moon River," which was written exclusively for her by Henry Mancini and Johnny Mercer and which she accompanies on guitar seated on a fire escape. The scene establishes Holly's underlying desire for simplicity and innocence in her life. During the preview, Paramount executive Martin Rackin exclaimed that the song had to go, whereupon Hepburn leaped up and, as her husband restrained her, replied angrily, "Over my dead body!" The song, of course, remained in the picture.[6] And for her efforts, she would earn her fourth Academy Award nomination, and "Moon River" would win for best song. Mancini credited the inspiration he received from Hepburn for the success of the ballad. He said in the late 1970s,

> It's unique for a composer to really be inspired by a person, a face or a personality. She not only inspired me to write "Moon River" but also "Charade" and "Two for the Road." If you listen to those songs you can almost tell who inspired them because they all have Audrey's quality of wistfulness—a kind of slight sadness.... when I met Audrey for the first time, I knew the song would be something very, very special. I knew the exact quality of her voice and that she could sing "Moon River" beautifully. To this day, no one has done it with more feeling or understanding.[7]

After spending time on location in New York, Audrey and Mel spent Christmas 1960 in Hollywood, as filming for *Breakfast at Tiffany's* wound down. Soon they were back in Burgenstock, though he left for long stretches to work on a film in Paris. Audrey reveled in the simplicity and peace of her life in Switzerland as a new mother. And she was soon to make a new friend in fellow actor Sophia Loren, who had moved to that country with her movie producer husband Carlos Ponti. Since both Mel and Carlos spent long stretches away, Audrey and Sophia, who also longed to have a child, spent a great deal of time together. They whiled away the hours talking and dining in Audrey's kitchen.

Those who believed the role of Holly Golightly ran against the grain in relation to Hepburn's personality were stunned when she accepted the part of lesbian teacher Karen Wright in *The Children's Hour*. The taboo subject was first broached in a play written by Lillian Hellman and performed on Broadway in 1934. A film adaptation titled *These Three* was created two years later, but the story was transformed into one of three heterosexuals involved in a love triangle. It was deemed that movie patrons were simply not ready to consume lesbianism along with their popcorn. William Wyler directed that film. And 24 years later, he wanted to try it again, this time tackling a subject that remained controversial in its time. He insisted that the remake would not be watered down.

Hepburn starred alongside Shirley MacLaine in *The Children's Hour*. She felt comfortable working with Wyler, who had directed her in *Roman Holiday*, but she also understood that playing a lesbian ran counter to her image. After all, she had just given birth and was considered the picture of femininity.

The film proved unsuccessful not because of the performances of Hepburn and MacLaine, but, according to the latter, due to a hesitance to take the plunge with the controversial subject matter. MacLaine, who played the role of Karen's lover Martha, believed Wyler was willing to dip his toes into the subject of homosexuality but was unwilling to dive right in. In fact, the word *lesbian* is never uttered in the film. MacLaine claimed that

> in the play, scenes were developed so that you could see Martha falling in love with Karen [but Wyler] thought they'd be too much for Middle America to take. I thought he was wrong, and I told him so, and Audrey was right behind me. But he was the director, and there was nothing we could do. Even so, I conceived my part as though those scenes were still there. I didn't want it to suddenly just hit her when the child tells the lie that maybe she could really be a lesbian....Lillian has

written a slow examination of one woman's personal growth
in the area of falling in love with another woman. But Willie
Wyler didn't want that.[8]

Perhaps Middle America wasn't ready. The usually enlightened movie
magazine *Films in Review* certainly wasn't, claiming that one scene in the
film, in which it is stated that lesbianism is not destructive, is disproved
by the number of lesbians who become insane or take their own lives.
But *The Children's Hour* received high marks from the industry, as five
Academy Award nominations attest. Though it took home no Oscars, the
attempt to take on the taboo subject was applauded.

A personal tragedy struck Hepburn, however, during her time filming
in Los Angeles. Her family was renting a home on Sunset Boulevard, from
which their Yorkie dog Famous escaped and raced into the street. Before
Audrey could track it down, she heard the sound of screeching tires and
yelping. The animal she cherished was dead. Though Mel quickly presented her with another dog, this time a Yorkshire terrier named Assam
of Assam, it took quite a while for the new pet to replace the old one in
her heart.

Following her work on *The Children's Hour*, Hepburn returned to Europe. Mel spent the next few months in Paris filming the World War II
epic *The Longest Day*. It was a plum assignment for him to be acting alongside such luminaries as John Wayne, Henry Fonda, Sean Connery, and
Robert Mitchum in a movie depicting the great Allied D-Day invasion,
but Audrey wanted nothing to do with violent war films, having experienced the violence of World War II herself. She merely wanted to relax at
Burgenstock and bond with Sean. Her primary consideration for accepting future roles would be geographical convenience. So she quickly signed
when offered a contract to perform in *Paris When It Sizzles*.

It was a major mistake. Her latest movie venture proved disappointing.
Costar William Holden had obviously not lost his feelings for Hepburn, a
fact that led to embarrassment. According to scriptwriter George Axel-
rod, Holden often showed up on the set drunk and, on one occasion,
even climbed a tree by a wall leading up to her room. Hepburn leaned out
the window to find out where the noise was coming from when Holden
grabbed and kissed her. He then slipped out of the tree and landed on a
parked car below, much to the dismay of his wife, Brenda. It took Holden
a week to return to the set.

Hepburn later admitted that her own insecurities didn't help matters.
She was going through a difficult period in her relationship with Mel, due
partly to their time apart, and the attention she received from Holden

brought positive reinforcement. But it also exacerbated Holden's problem and jeopardized the entire project.

To the surprise of no one, the film was universally panned. Hepburn later called it her worst film experience. But she was facing more critical problems. Her marriage was beginning to crumble.

## NOTES

1. Diana Maychick, *Audrey Hepburn: An Intimate Portrait* (New York: Carol, 1993), 137.

2. Barry Paris, *Audrey Hepburn* (New York: G. P. Putnam's Sons, 1996), 152.

3. Henry Hart, "Forever Silence," *Films in Review* 10, no. 6 (1959): 353.

4. Paris, *Audrey Hepburn,* 165.

5. Donald Spoto, *Enchantment: The Life of Audrey Hepburn* (New York: Harmony Books, 2006), 202.

6. Ibid., 205.

7. Sean Hepburn Ferrer, *Audrey Hepburn: An Elegant Spirit* (New York: Atria Books, 2003), 83.

8. Vito Russo, *The Celluloid Closet: Homosexuality in the Movies* (New York: Harper & Row, 1981), 139.

# Chapter 8

# MY FAIR LADY

As Hepburn strolled around in New York, then near her home in Switzerland in 1960, she felt somebody following her. She knew she had seen the young man more than once in both countries, and an eerie sensation washed over her. She wondered if it was merely her imagination, so she kept it a secret.

She began to fear the man. She considered confronting him but feared the worst consequences if he was indeed dangerous. She was already a bundle of nerves in her private and public lives. The perceived stalker simply made her more so.

Eventually, her fears were proven justified. During her filming of *Paris When It Sizzles*, word came in from Burgenstock that a 22-year-old science student named Jean-Claude Thouroude had turned himself in for breaking and entering her home. He had stolen her Oscar for *Roman Holiday*. He had written her so many fan letters that her secretary didn't bother passing them on to her.

The relief she felt when the stalker had been removed from her life was about the only positive development that emerged from her work on the ill-fated *Paris When It Sizzles*. But it always seemed during her career that a flop was followed by a hit. And the comedy thriller *Charade* was certainly a hit.

Veteran actor and one-time heartthrob Cary Grant was approached with the script about a young widow whom his character would help discover that her husband had been a crook. After Grant read the script, he exclaimed that Hepburn would be perfect for the role. When Hepburn read the script, she remarked that Grant would be ideal for that part. It was a match made in Hollywood heaven. And with such actors as Walter Matthau, George Kennedy, and James Coburn in the film, it could hardly fail. Though Grant was 25 years her senior and her designs on him in the film hardly seemed plausible, it went off without a hitch. And while *Paris When It Sizzles* was bombing at the box office and being lambasted by critics, *Charade* was receiving both public and critical success.

But though Hepburn enjoyed working with Grant, there was one film she leaped at the opportunity in which to star: *My Fair Lady.* She was well aware that the Broadway play produced in 1956 was being prepared for the silver screen, and she had never been as enthusiastic about a potential role as that of the poor cockney flower girl who is transformed into a proper woman by stuffy professor of phonetics Henry Higgins. Julie Andrews, who later starred in such movie classic musicals as *Mary Poppins* and *The Sound of Music*, had performed that role of Eliza Doolittle in the play on Broadway, then also repeated the success in London two years later. In 1960, Hepburn expressed her desire to land that part. "I ought to campaign for it, I suppose," she had said. "There's no other role I'm dying to do. I must be Eliza."[1]

Andrews, however, was considered by many a shoo-in to land the part in the movie, and Hepburn was neither one to fight for what she wished for professionally nor one to ace someone out of a role that seemed rightfully hers. So she made it clear that she wanted the part of Eliza and simply awaited word on her request.

As it turned out, Hepburn was the shoo-in. Producer Jack L. Warner had spent a king's ransom for the film rights, and he needed an established movie star to attract huge audiences. Andrews had far more experience in the theater than in film. Hepburn's agent Kurt Frings began negotiations with Warner Bros., which had paid CBS Television a record sum of 5.5 million dollars for the rights to *My Fair Lady.* And when all had signed on the dotted lines, Hepburn was to be paid 1 million dollars in seven installments stretched out for six years beginning on July 1, 1963. That was five times the amount earned by costar Rex Harrison, who had been Warner's second choice for the part of Henry Higgins behind Peter O'Toole. O'Toole had simply asked for too much money up front as well as a large percentage of the box office earnings.

Andrews handled the disappointment of being passed over for the part quite well, but she issued a warning to Hepburn that the singing parts, particularly for songs such as "I Could Have Danced All Night" and "Just You Wait, Enery Iggins," were quite difficult. Though Andrews didn't claim Hepburn wasn't up to the task, she left that up to speculation. And when Hepburn asked director George Cukor if he was indeed going to use her voice in the film, he replied that he would only if she proved herself worthy.

Hepburn didn't feel she would be maximizing her experience or performance by losing the opportunity to sing. She toiled diligently with a voice coach, but it seemed to be a losing battle. She was informed that the director had taken the precaution of having professional opera singer, Marni Nixon, record all the songs from the film. Nixon had been used to dub over Deborah Kerr in *The King and I* and Natalie Wood in *West Side Story*, so though she was told that the decision to use Nixon's voice rather than her own had yet to be made, Hepburn feared that such encouragement was used only to prevent her from losing her enthusiasm.

That fear was justified. Hepburn continued to work on her voice, despite the fact that a commitment to Nixon had already been made. When it finally came to light, Hepburn felt betrayed, but she refused to allow it to affect her performance. Many to this day, however, believe, in listening to still surviving recordings of Hepburn singing such *My Fair Lady* classics as "Wouldn't It Be Loverly," that her own voice would have proven more than adequate for the film, though Nixon's mastery of all the songs cannot be disputed. And it is also widely believed that the decision to scrap the idea of using Hepburn's own voice cost her an Academy Award nomination. After all, how could she win the ultimate prize for performing in a musical in which she never sang?

Hepburn's daily routine during the filming of *My Fair Lady* included an hour of "dirtying up" in making her a presentable flower girl, a chore that included placing dirt into her fingernails and onto her face. Making matters more difficult was the heat wave that struck the San Fernando Valley, where the film was being shot. Temperatures soared to well over 100 degrees, which made it quite uncomfortable for Hepburn, who was adorned, as Eliza, in heavy wool skirts. She didn't even receive relief by starting work at 5:00 A.M. due to the blast of hot desert air that hit the area at sunrise. And the theft of her wedding ring from her bag in her dressing room added to the trauma.

The experience frayed Hepburn emotionally. Doctors ordered her to take a three-day break from filming on November 19, 1963. And on the day she returned, a cataclysmic event served to minimize the importance of every aspect of her personal and professional life. As she discussed a scene with Cukor, someone with a portable radio raced up with the news that President John F. Kennedy had been assassinated in Dallas. Neither the badly shaken Cukor nor anyone else in on the news could summon the courage to announce the tragedy. So Hepburn grabbed a microphone, informed the crew of Kennedy's death, and requested two minutes of silence, after which she muttered, "May God have mercy on us all."[2] She had taken the difficult chore on herself because of a British theater tradition that called for the leading man or leading woman to make any special announcements to the company.

The film was released in the fall of 1964. Though some in the British press chided what they considered to be her inadequate Cockney accent, legendary British actor John Gielgud praised her performance, comparing it favorably with that of Andrews. And American journalists chimed in as well: "Miss Hepburn brings a fine sensitivity of feeling and phenomenal histrionic skill [to the role]," wrote *New York Times* critic Bosley Crowther. "She is dazzlingly beautiful and comic in the crisply satiric Ascot scene, stiffly serene and distant at the embassy ball, and almost unbearably poignant in the latter scenes when she hungers for love."[3]

Eliza indeed hungered for love in *My Fair Lady*. But the love between Audrey and Mel had little opportunity to be cultivated. The fact that she was now one of the most beloved actors in film history, while he had long been dismissed inside and outside the business, placed a strain on their relationship. So did the geographic distance between them. But she continued to work feverishly to keep the foundering marriage alive. Rather than take a well-deserved rest, she took 16 trips in eight months to Europe to visit Mel, where he had been involved in several poorly received movies. On one particular excursion to Spain, she stayed with him on location in miserable conditions. The woman who had earned 1 million dollars to portray Eliza Doolittle was now living in primitive villages, choking down barely edible food and sleeping in discomfort just to remain close to her husband.

During that same trip, Hepburn learned that she had not been nominated for an Academy Award for her performance in *My Fair Lady*. To add insult to injury, Rex Harrison (whose poor singing voice had forced him to talk through his singing parts) had been nominated for his role in that same film, and Andrews had been selected for playing the title character in *Mary Poppins*. But she handled the disappointment with remarkable aplomb, even presenting the best actor Oscar to Harrison during the ceremonies and congratulating Andrews when she won the award for best actress. She also admitted that she herself was disappointed by her portrayal of a Cockney flower girl early in the picture, but received some solace that *My Fair Lady* won best picture, which she believed to be at least a bit of a tribute to her. And though she expressed no resentment toward Andrews, she did believe politics played a part in the proceedings.

"I was delighted for [Andrews]," Hepburn said. "I really was. But everybody else was even more thrilled. I think the world perceived her win as some sort of divine justice, and I think I wasn't nominated because they wanted to punish me because she didn't get the part. I realized something then, that it's always better to be thought of as the underdog, and never the winner. The thing is, I always felt like the underdog. For my whole career, I felt like the underdog."[4]

Soon she and Mel bought a house along the sandy beaches of southeastern Spain, which would allow them to spend more time together when he was working in that country. They also made a momentous decision that was intended to strengthen their marriage and provide roots for Sean, who had spent the first four years of his life traveling endlessly. They took steps to leave her beloved Burgenstock, where, if they had remained, Sean would have been forced to attend a German school. Instead, they scoured the country and purchased a home on the other side of Switzerland. They found a simple, two-story, sixteenth-century farmhouse in the remote village of Tolochenaz, which overlooked the Alps and boasted a population of just 450, most of whom were farmers. The home brought a simplicity and wholesomeness that his mother very much desired for him. And Sean recalled those early days of his life with fondness:

> My friends were the sons and daughters of farmers and school-teachers. There was an orphanage down the road, and those children were my friends too. I remember being awakened in the middle of the night by one of my school chums. One of the father's cows was giving birth. I can still feel the cold air whipping my face as we ran, in the middle of the night, under the train tracks to catch this most wonderful event. Another friend, my best friend, lived in the house whose garden touched ours. We carved a passage through the hedge and spent hours in his attic playing with an old train set that had been built by his father and perfected by his older brother.[5]

Audrey reveled in her role as stay-home mom after the house in Tolochenaz had been purchased. But she could never resist Paris, and when she was offered an opportunity to star in the light comedy *How to Steal a Million*, which would be shot there, she jumped at the opportunity to work with director William Wyler for the third time in her career. She would play the daughter of an art forger who creates a perfect fake of a statue that is about to go on exhibit as the original. Worried that her father will be arrested, she teams up with a burglar, portrayed by Peter O'Toole, to steal the phony.

The film was not only a commercial success, but it also proved that Hepburn could thrive acting in the faster-paced comedies of the 1960s.

She had also been redefined in her mid-thirties as a performer who could act her age and even play roles as a woman who was older than the leading man. Her performance in *How to Steal a Million* led to an offer to play a sexy wife in an adulterous marriage in the sophisticated comedy *Two for the Road,* and another to play a blind woman tormented by a vicious criminal in the taut thriller *Wait until Dark.* She accepted both roles, which showed her expanding range as an actor.

Her personal life, however, was not as rosy. She was thrilled to learn in December 1965 that she was again pregnant, greatly because she had hoped Sean would not grow up without a sibling. She also believed another child would strengthen a marriage that seemed to be teetering on the brink of collapse. Mel had not joined her in Paris as she worked on *How to Steal a Million,* and he had been spending less time with her in recent months. He had been negotiating new roles for her with Warner Bros., but it seemed their relationship had deteriorated to the point where it was more professional than romantic. And when she suffered another miscarriage in January 1966, she slipped into a depression.

Meanwhile, both *Two for the Road* and *Wait until Dark* earned critical acclaim. Her role as Joanna in the former was a tremendous departure for her, and it brought her frighteningly into focus about her own life. Though Audrey was concerned over press reports of Mel's alleged infidelity, it was not the extramarital affairs in the film that she felt paralleled the situation in her marriage, but rather, the overall destruction of the relationship. Young Albert Finney, who was six years her junior, played Joanna's husband in the movie. Audrey was enraptured by Finney's youthful exuberance and carefree outlook on life. They began a romance that would signal the end of her marriage with Mel, who eventually learned of their affair.

According to Hepburn biographer Daniel Spoto, some who knew the couple reported that Mel warned Audrey that if she didn't end her relationship with Finney, he would file for divorce and cite her adultery as the catalyst. Despite reports of Mel's infidelities, she had no proof. And she was frightened that if it was indeed learned that she was having an affair with Finney, the courts could rule her to be an unfit mother and give sole custody of Sean to Mel. The romance thus ended. Sean, after all, had become the primary reason Audrey hoped to keep her marriage alive. And the young boy sensed trouble. "I remember there was a tension in my parents' marriage at that time," Sean said. "Only years later did I realize it was because she was having an affair with Finney during the making of that movie."[6]

The eerie similarities between Hepburn's current feelings and experiences in relation to her marriage and those of Joanna in *Two for the*

*Road* allowed her to act with tremendous realism, conviction, and emotional depth. Director Stanley Donen called it the best performance of her career, but the American public was simply not ready for the dramatic change in her image. The film struggled in the United States but fared better in Europe, where films depicting marital problems had gained greater acceptance and were far more commonplace.

*Wait until Dark*, for which Hepburn again earned a salary of 1 million dollars, presented different challenges. She studied with physician Wilhelm Streiff, who specialized in working with the blind. She worked with a blind college student named Karen Goldstein. She wore a blinder mask especially designed for patients who were losing their sight. She learned to touch surfaces with realism and to listen to various sound levels to judge their closeness or distance. She learned to walk with a cane. She had to learn the simplest of tasks all over again, such as drinking tea without rattling the cup or spilling. Hepburn gained a tremendous appreciation for what the blind must overcome in their daily lives. It was painstaking, but rewarding, and it proved fascinating to her.

*Wait until Dark* gave Audrey the opportunity to work again with her husband, who produced the film. But at that point in their relationship, closeness merely exacerbated their marital problems. In addition, she missed Sean terribly. The rigors of performing such a difficult role and the challenges of her personal life combined to cause her to lose 15 pounds during the filming, which she requested in vain be done in Europe so that she could be close to her son. In July 1967, she became pregnant, but lost yet another child the following month. She had fooled herself into thinking a second baby would save her marriage, but when it was gone, so were all her hopes.

In September, just before the release of *Wait until Dark*, the couple filed for divorce. They had simply grown too far apart. Though opinions vary as to why it eventually fizzled, all agree that their professional relationship played a major role. Actor Yul Brynner believed Mel's male ego got in the way. He wondered, in fact, how Audrey held out as long as she did. "I suppose she was desperate to make it work [and] so sweet, loyal and human," he said. "Mel was jealous of her success and could not reconcile himself to the [fact that] she was much better than he in every way, and he took it out on her. Finally, she couldn't take it any longer. God knows, she did everything a woman could do to save her marriage."[7]

Even Ferrer admitted that jealousy got the better of him. "It's a problem when the wife outshines the husband as Audrey does me," he said with admirable candor in 1960. "I'm pretty sensitive when producers call and say they want to discuss a film with me, when in reality they're angling for Audrey and using me as bait."[8]

*Wait until Dark* opened in November 1967 and grossed a whopping 11 million dollars. It also resulted in a fifth Oscar nomination for Hepburn, who was miserable anyway. She had the unenviable task of breaking the news of the divorce to Sean, whom she simply told that she and his father were no longer happy together. Audrey refused to express any negative thoughts she had about Mel to her son. And she did everything in her power to ensure that the relationship between Sean and his dad would remain fruitful. The breakup itself was performed amicably. Neither bad-mouthed the other publicly.

Those close to Audrey believed she was never the same emotionally after the divorce. She firmly believed in "til death do you part." She had vowed, greatly because of the traumatic divorce of her own parents, to remain wed for the sake of Sean and the sanctity of marriage, but it was all in vain.

"I thought a marriage between two good, loving people had to last until one of them died," she told journalist Henry Gris. "I can't really tell you how disillusioned I was. I tried and I tried. I knew how difficult it [was to be] second-billed on the screen and in real life. How Mel suffered! But believe me, I put my career second. [Even] when it was clear the marriage was ending, I still couldn't let go."[9]

What Audrey did let go was her career, at least temporarily. She informed agent Kurt Frings to stop sending her scripts. She would have only one career now. And that would be the mother of her only child.

## NOTES

1. Alexander Walker, *Audrey: Her Real Story* (New York: St. Martin's Griffin, 1994), 184.

2. David Lewin, "The Most Exciting Girl in the World," *London Daily Mail*, October 24, 1964.

3. Bosley Crowther, *New York Times*, October 22, 1964.

4. Diana Maychick, *Audrey Hepburn: An Intimate Portrait* (New York: Carol, 1993), 185–86.

5. Sean Hepburn Ferrer, *Audrey Hepburn: An Elegant Spirit* (New York: Atria Books, 2003), 138.

6. Donald Spoto, *Enchantment: The Life of Audrey Hepburn* (New York: Harmony Books, 2006), 253.

7. Warren Harris, *Audrey Hepburn* (New York: Simon & Schuster, 1994), 216.

8. Barry Paris, *Audrey Hepburn* (New York: G. P. Putnam's Sons, 1996), 240.

9. Charles Higham, *Audrey: The Life of Audrey Hepburn* (New York: Macmillan, 1984), 190.

# Chapter 9

# NEW LIFE FOR AUDREY

Solitude was never an enemy to Audrey. So when she retreated to her Tolochenaz home in 1967, one might believe she would emotionally recover quickly from her breakup. And she always had Sean to dote on, which would serve to keep her mind off the divorce.

It worked better in theory than in practice. By the fall, Sean was off to school, which left Audrey alone to contemplate what went wrong. Not only did she place blame on herself, but she also became lonely. Now available again, she enjoyed the company of men, including Spanish prince Alfonso de Bourbon-Dampierre, with whom she spent New Year's Eve in Madrid. But Audrey was simply not ready to move on romantically.

By the summer of 1968, Audrey felt she had to get away. She accepted an invitation to join Princess Olympia Torlonia and her millionaire husband Paul Weiller on an Aegean Sea cruise of the Greek islands. Among the passengers was 30-year-old Dr. Andrea Mario Dotti, a handsome young Italian psychiatrist who was bred in tremendous wealth. Audrey experienced an immediate attraction to the charming Dotti, as did he for her.

If it's important that a couple have a tale to tell about their initial meeting—a story to enjoy and embellish in later years—Audrey and Andrea had one. Andrea told her that at the age of 14, he had seen her in *Roman Holiday* and had become enraptured by her. In fact, he had informed his mother that he was going to marry the beautiful actor someday. As he reached puberty, he was motivated to attend every movie in which she starred. He went on to tell Audrey that he had met her at a party in the 1950s and attempted to make his feelings known through his gaze and his gestures toward her, but they were either not deciphered or ignored. She replied that she remembered neither him nor the occasion.

Audrey not only told friends that Andrea had vastly improved her frame of mind, but also that she was even in love with the man who was nine years her junior. He had charmed her out of the depression with which she had suffered since the demise of her marriage, placing her in a far better mood when she returned to Switzerland in the fall of 1968 to finalize the divorce. The courtship was swift and decisive. She and Andrea spent a great deal of time in his native Italy. Their most romantic encounters were at his friend's cottage on the island of Giglio, where they spent many weekends. And on Christmas Eve of that year, he presented her with a solitaire diamond engagement ring from Bulgaria. Despite the dizzying rapidity with which their relationship blossomed, Audrey quickly accepted his proposal.

Andrea, too, was a product of divorce. His father abandoned Andrea and his three brothers during Andrea's childhood, a lamentable fact with which Audrey could identify. His mother, Signora Paula Roberti, recalled her son speaking often about getting married and having many children, but added that his career had always taken precedence, until he returned from the cruise with Audrey, after which love was in his eyes and in his heart.

Her awareness of Andrea's passion for Audrey played a role in Paula's own love for her. She was only 14 years older than Audrey, which also gave them a bit more in common. The two spent a great deal of time together in the kitchen, where Paula taught Audrey the finer points of Italian cooking, a hobby the now semiretired actor thoroughly enjoyed. Paula was so taken with Audrey that she offered the couple two floors of her own estate in which to live. They declined the invitation, however, opting instead for a penthouse that overlooked Rome.

It was not, however, as if she no longer had a care in the world. She worried about how the newfound fame would affect Andrea and if he could hold up to the media scrutiny. But he considered it no problem, expressing his naive view that he would never become a public figure and, in fact, didn't even think of his wife as an actor. Soon, however, difficulties did arise. It became apparent that Andrea, who had readily admitted to being enamored with Audrey as a young teenager, had embraced the notion of being married to a celebrity. He not only approved interviews with the media, but he also didn't discourage the occasional paparazzi that somehow found their way to their doorstep. He even went so far as to offer to one journalist that "she is a great actress, and it would be criminal to deprive her of something she loves."[1] Audrey, of course, was being deprived of nothing but peace and quiet. Her departure from acting had been self-imposed. Her desire at the time was to sleep in, take care of Sean, and relax.

And in June 1969, she became pregnant yet again and returned to her beloved Switzerland for solitude. This time she delivered, but not without some anxious moments. Audrey was so determined to avoid another miscarriage that she spent the last 10 weeks of her pregnancy in bed. And on February 8, 1970, she indeed gave birth through a caesarian delivery to son Luca. Though she wanted to continue having children and yearned for a daughter, doctors advised against tempting fate.

In an attempt to avoid the media and maintain the quiet life she so desired, Audrey returned for long stretches of time to Switzerland with her two children, while Andrea remained in Rome. Newspaper photos showed him often surrounded by young, attractive women in nightclubs, whom he claimed to be working associates. But then, he often frequented discos without his wife when she was in Rome, though Audrey's close friend Robert Wolders claimed she was humiliated at seeing the pictures of Andrea partying with attractive women. Andrea denied any unfaithfulness, and none was proven at that time.

A new chapter in Audrey's life was beginning, not merely as a result of her second child. In the fall of 1970, she was asked by a representative of the United Nations Children's Fund (UNICEF), with which she had been so impressed from her experiences at the end of World War II, to appear in a Christmas special on TV to help raise funds for the organization. She would be shown simply singing with a group of poverty-stricken youngsters in New York on a program titled A World of Love, hosted by Bill Cosby and Shirley MacLaine. Audrey eagerly agreed, and three days before Christmas, she was seen in America for the first time in three years. The event planted the seeds of a relationship between Audrey and UNICEF that would last the rest of her life.

Meanwhile, the offers continued to pour in. She was offered one million dollars to play the part of a Russian tsarina in Nicholas and Alexandra and considered it, but she read the script and turned it down. It was a wise decision—the film was a financial and critical flop. At least she thought over the possibility of performing in that movie. She simply sent most scripts back unread. And she answered critics who claimed that acting was her calling. "I've never believed in this God-given talent," she told journalist Henry Gris. "I adored my work and I did my best. I don't think I'm robbing anybody of anything and I think I would be robbing my family, you know, my husband and two divine children, of the attention they should get. Otherwise, there's no point in having a wife and mother.... I have no desire to work."[2]

Audrey indeed put endless energy into those roles. Though she had the benefits of a staff at her disposal, she woke at 5:30 A.M. to arrange flowers or do other busy work in the garden before awakening Sean. She would often help with the cooking and would also help with Sean's homework, read to both kids, and escort them to the movies or chauffeur them to the homes of friends. Audrey enjoyed dressing down for all occasions and showed a down-to-earth personality to all with whom she came in contact. And, as always, she rejected all offers to return to work, except one. She accepted more than one million dollars to shoot a series of TV commercials at a Rome studio for a Tokyo-based wig manufacturer in early 1972.

It seemed nothing could pique her interest to return to the screen. She accompanied her husband to New York in 1973 and spent time with actor Marian Seldes, whom she hadn't seen since the two performed together in the play *Ondine* nearly 20 years earlier. But rather than talk about acting, they swapped stories about motherhood. Speculation ran rampant that the trip to the United States signaled the rebirth of her movie career, but she stated simply and truthfully that she was accompanying Andrea to a medical convention. She told journalists in no uncertain terms that she never felt part of the Hollywood scene, that despite rumors to the contrary, her marriage was wonderful, and that she was quite content being an Italian housewife.

Her sentiments were not about to change. During an interview nearly three years later, when Sean had risen to six foot three and was 15 years old, and Luca was attending kindergarten, she spoke of the unbridled joy she felt and even criticized the changes in content and subject matter that had permeated the movie industry since she had last appeared in a film in 1967. Gone, it seemed, were the comparatively tame films that hinted at sex and shunned explicit scenes of violence:

> The happiest I've ever been has been in the seventies. I'm much less restless now, and no longer searching for the wrong values.... I've had so much more than I ever dreamed possible out of life—[no] great disappointments or hopes that didn't work out; I didn't expect anything much and because of that I'm the least bitter woman I know.... I've accomplished far more than I ever hoped to, and most of the time it happened without my seeking it.... I'm glad to have missed what's happening in the movies these last eight years. It's all been sex and violence, and I'm far too scrawny to strip and I hate guns, so I'm better off out of it.[3]

By that time, however, Hepburn was indeed strongly considering a new project titled *Robin and Marian,* a screenplay that spotlighted a middle-aged Robin Hood and Maid Marian years after their swashbuckling youth. The rather far-fetched but humorous plot features a Robin Hood that has returned from the Crusades quite battered and beaten and a Marian who has been transformed into a nun. Meanwhile, the evil sheriff of Nottingham still searches Sherwood Forest to exact revenge for past deeds on Robin and his merry men, who include the still surviving Friar Tuck and Little John.

Director Richard Lester flew to Europe to convince Hepburn to participate. He promised to have her parts shot during the kids' summer vacation, which would allow her to bring them with her to location in Spain, and further assured her that Sean and Luca would return in time for fall classes. Though leery about her own appearance after eight years away from show business and dreading the inevitability of once again being forced to be an extrovert, which was certainly against her grain, she agreed to take on the part.

Hepburn worried that the filming would extend past its schedule, thereby robbing her of time with her kids once September rolled around. Gratefully, it lasted a mere six weeks. But during the filming, Andrea suffered a scare in Rome that shook Audrey and convinced her that the safest and best place to raise their kids would be Tolochenaz. One day, four men wearing ski masks attempted to drag Andrea from his parked Mercedes. He fought back but was beaten badly and incurred severe cuts and bruises. Security personnel from the nearby Egyptian Embassy stopped the attack, and Andrea was able to contact Audrey with news of the incident before the media informed her.

The star-studded cast in *Robin and Marian* included Robert Shaw, fresh off of starring in the blockbuster *Jaws,* as well as Sean Connery, who had gained fame by playing James Bond. But despite the inclusion of such accomplished actors, the film received mixed reviews and only mild success at the box office, though both the public and media welcomed Hepburn back to the screen.

Meanwhile, Audrey was becoming increasingly concerned about the photos of Andrea enjoying the company of scantily dressed women in nightclubs, which were appearing in various European tabloids. Though Andrea maintained to his wife that the young ladies were merely friends, she remained suspicious. She declined to seek a divorce, at least partly for the sake of their children. Sean believed, however, that his mother took a rather weak approach to what he believed to be his stepfather's infidelities and that Andrea was, simply, a bit of a cad.

"What she needed to do was speak up and be heard when she needed to, and she didn't put up healthy boundaries," Sean said. "My stepfather was a brilliant and funny psychiatrist—but he was a hound dog. He just didn't know how to be faithful. Not a good choice of husband if what you are looking for is security."[4] And Andrea later admitted, "I was no angel. Italian husbands have never been famous for being faithful."[5] The final indignity was when Audrey learned that her husband had taken women to their home for romantic interludes on more than one occasion.

Though she continued to tell the media that her marriage was sound, the handwriting was on the wall by the spring of 1978. But as was her tendency, she blamed herself for her marriage's failures and even, to a great extent, for Andrea's trysts with the opposite sex. She fell into a deep depression, arguably the most severe in a life that had been peppered with lengthy emotional bouts of emotional turmoil. It was a cue to throw herself back into her work, which she did when she was offered a part in the movie *Bloodline*, to be directed by old friend Terence Young, whom she had met when he was a young British paratrooper in 1944 and who later directed her in *Wait until Dark*. The prospect of reuniting with Young and a desire to alleviate her emotional troubles motivated Hepburn to accept the role in a movie with questionable potential. And the million-dollar salary for performing in the film certainly added to the attraction.

Another bonus was that Hepburn was promised that she would work three-week stretches, which would allow her to visit Sean and Luca often. The former had been enrolled at a Swiss university, while the latter was attending grammar school in Rome. The filming would take her there as well as New York and Paris. In *Bloodline*, Hepburn portrayed a 23-year-old woman who inherits a pharmaceutical house and is threatened with murder by a number of criminals with various motives. The plotline was a bit of a stretch, and so was the fact that she would be playing a woman barely half her age.

Perhaps the only memorable aspect to Hepburn's experience filming *Bloodline* was her relationship with costar Ben Gazzara, who has since expressed his feeling that the two felt chemistry on their first meeting. Audrey shed her usual inhibitions and approached Gazzara, who was still married to fellow actor Janice Rule. Gazzara was reading a book at the time and blandly stated that the activity helped him sleep. She replied that she, too, had been having problems falling asleep and that he should call her if he experienced any more sleepless nights. Soon thereafter, they met for lunch, during which she poured her heart out, complaining to her new friend that her husband had not only been untrue, but also that he had chosen their own home as his personal hotel room for affairs. Hepburn and Gazzara soon consummated their relationship. They continued their romance at the Hotel Crillon in Paris in what he described as "a night filled with far more feeling than any other we'd had together."[6]

Soon, however, Gazzara was on his way to Korea to star in another film to be directed by Young, in which Sean was to be used as a production assistant. Audrey thus believed there were two reasons to visit Korea, but she was hurt when Gazzara discouraged her from joining him. He was at the time beginning a relationship with Elke Stuckmann, who would eventually become his third wife. Audrey awaited his return to Rome, whereupon she asked again to see him, but he declined.

"Obviously I wasn't in love," he explained later. "I was flattered that someone like that would be in love with me. But I didn't know how deeply she was in love with me until I left her. She told others, not me, that I had broken her heart. She was so kind and sweet. And I hurt her."[7]

She would soon be hurt again by the reaction of critics and the public to *Bloodline*, which was universally panned. But both Gazzara and Hepburn would be given an opportunity to redeem themselves when director Peter Bogdanovich asked both to perform in *They All Laughed*. Gazzara had told Bogdanovich in detail about his relationship with Hepburn, which the director used as inspiration to work her role in the film. She played a woman passionately dedicated to her young son who remains steadfast, despite a cheating husband, before experiencing an intense fling of her own with a detective whom the husband had hired to keep an eye on her.

When Hepburn learned that Gazzara would be her costar, she quickly signed yet another million-dollar contract with great anticipation that working so close to the man for whom she had designs would again spark a romance. And Sean was again hired as a personal assistant, which would prove to be another inducement for Hepburn. In early 1980, however, an encounter with Gazzara convinced her that the relationship was indeed over, whereupon she recanted her commitment to *They All Laughed*. But she realized that such an action would ruin the film for everyone, including Sean, so she again agreed to participate in the filming, which was carried out that spring and early summer. What Gazzara didn't know was that by the time the 50-year-old Audrey arrived on the set, she had found another man.

## NOTES

1. Julia Kay, "Audrey Hepburn," *Photoplay*, April 1969, 76.

2. Charles Higham, *Audrey: The Life of Audrey Hepburn* (New York: Macmillan, 1984), 200.

3. Quoted in Rex Reed, "Our Fair Lady Is Back, and It's Spring," *New York Sunday News*, March 21, 1976.

4. Sean Hepburn Ferrer, *Audrey Hepburn: An Elegant Spirit* (New York: Atria Books, 2003), 13.

5. J. D. Podolsky, "Life with Audrey," *People Magazine*, October 31, 1994.

6. Ben Gazzara, *In the Moment: My Life as an Actor* (New York: Carroll & Graf, 2004), 191.

7. Ben Gazzara, interview with Edward Guthmann, *San Francisco Chronicle*, November 18, 2004.

# Chapter 10

# OLD FAN, NEW MAN

The new man in Audrey's life was Robert Wolders, a regular on the popular TV western *Laredo*, to whom she had been introduced at a Christmas party in 1979. They had much in common, including Dutch heritage. The dashing Wolders had been married to actor Merle Oberon, who was 25 years his senior. But Oberon had died on Thanksgiving Day at the age of 68. Neither was in a mood for romance when they met. He was just beginning to get over the death of his wife, and Audrey was still lamenting her divorce and unhappy marriage to Andrea. But misery loves company, and it was a bonus that they could communicate with each other in their native Dutch language as well as in English. In the spring of 1980, when Audrey was in New York during the filming of *They All Laughed*, he called her from Los Angeles. Wolders flew to the Big Apple and the romance began. He felt strongly enough about Audrey to soon move to Switzerland to be near her.

When Audrey returned to Rome, she had some news for her philandering husband. Andrea noticed her beaming expression and blurted out, "You look very beautiful—you must be in love." Throwing caution to the wind, Audrey replied, "I am!"[1] It was painfully apparent by that time that the marriage was over. Though most blamed Andrea and his infidelities for its failures, others have noted that Audrey's constant state of depression also played a role.

Audrey certainly needed the companionship of Wolders because other areas of her personal life were far less encouraging. Her brother Alexander had died in 1978 at the age of 58 from a freak electrical accident at his home in Spain. And not only was her relationship with Andrea nearly destroyed, but her mother Ella suffered her third stroke in July 1980. Audrey spent a great deal of time trying to nurse her back to health. She introduced Rob to Ella, who was far more impressed with her daughter's new beau than she had been with either of her two husbands.

Rob was the ideal complement for Audrey. He, too, enjoyed the quiet, contemplative life. The couple would rise early, eat a light breakfast, enjoy working in the garden, shop at the local market, and take pleasant walks together with their Jack Russell terriers. They watched tapes of their favorite TV shows together before retiring well before midnight. Only professional commitments would lure either one to America or other areas of Europe.

However, the United States was certainly not where Audrey wanted to be when *They All Laughed* was released. Just weeks after the shooting had concluded, Bogdanovich had suffered a personal tragedy: aspiring actor and 1980 *Playboy Magazine* Playmate of the Year Dorothy Stratten was shot and killed by her jealous husband, who then turned the gun on himself. Two weeks earlier, she had left her husband to move in with Bogdanovich. Not only was Bogdanovich devastated by the news, but the resulting publicity also proved damaging to the distribution process of the film.

That rather sad turn of events would be followed by yet another. Audrey learned early in 1981 that her father's health was also failing. Robert accompanied her to Dublin to see her father, whom she hadn't visited since the ill-fated trip 22 years earlier. But his distant behavior toward his daughter remained, so she left after two days. Ruston was dead a week later. Not a single obituary was written; his Fascist past had been neither forgotten nor forgiven. By 1984, both of Audrey's parents were gone. Though she could hardly be expected to miss a father who had abandoned his family when she was young and who had made no effort to patch their relationship, she was quite distraught at the loss of Ella. Granted, she had never received the praise and emotional support from her mother that she so desired, but Audrey felt an emptiness following her death that remained with her the rest of her life.

"I was lost without my mother," Audrey said. "She had been my sounding board, my conscience. She was not the most affectionate person—in fact there were times when I thought she was cold—but she loved me in her heart, and I knew that all along. I never got that feeling from my father, unfortunately."[2]

Robert had moved in with Audrey well before her divorce had been finalized. Andrea was balking over the custody of Luca, insisting that his son remain with him in Rome while he attended school. But despite the fact that Andrea had caused so much emotional pain for his wife, Robert was taken aback by the fact that he never heard Audrey make one derogatory comment about her husband. The divorce finally became official in 1982, after which Andrea never again wed. Neither did Audrey, who had sworn off marriage by that time. Whenever she was asked when she was going to marry Robert, she quickly replied that she and her beau were quite content with the status quo. Robert understood, quipping that Audrey getting married after her experiences with Mel and Andrea would be akin to someone returning to the electric chair after having just been seated on it.

Though Hepburn was now essentially retired from the movie business, publicist and writer Eleanor Lambert offered a project in 1981 that she believed the film legend might embrace. Lambert handled the account for Tiffany's, and when the jewelry store was planning an expansion, she deemed Hepburn to be the perfect spokesperson for the event and guest of honor at the opening of the new branches. Hepburn agreed but quickly changed her mind. She had shied away from the notion of appearing extensively again in public.

Hepburn did, however, appear that same year at an American Film Institute tribute to Cary Grant, for which she wrote a special lyrical poem for the occasion. Grant wept after the poem was read, even as he was shown embracing President Ronald Reagan and first lady Nancy.

Always introspective and sensitive, Hepburn was deeply saddened by the illnesses and deaths of her relatives, but also of close friends. William Wyler passed away in 1983. Playwright Noel Coward, whom she had visited often in Paris, was suffering from Lou Gehrig's disease in the early 1980s. Esteemed actor David Niven, who had comforted her after she had witnessed a suicide early in her career, died at the age of 74 in August 1983. The seemingly endless bad news seemed to take a toll on the usually polite Hepburn, even in social situations. Designer Jeffrey Banks, who had been smitten with Hepburn ever since he had seen her in *Funny Face*, spoke about the letdown he had experienced in May 1983 when he met her for the first time. "I was a little disappointed," he said. "She was perfectly cordial but she seemed distant. It wasn't the magical moment I had created in my head."[3]

The personal tragedies drew Audrey closer to Sean. Now blossoming in the field of film production, her older son had married Italian designer Marina Spadafora. The couple was wed in Los Angeles in a ceremony in which both Audrey and Mel were seen together for the first time since their divorce. Audrey bought them a 375,000-dollar home as a wedding gift, but they didn't occupy the home for very long. In fact, Sean and Marina were divorced four years later.

Though Hepburn's film career would never be reborn, she did accept her only TV movie role in 1986. Directed by Roger Young, *Love among Thieves* was a romantic mystery that costarred Robert Wagner, who had been thriving in that medium for a generation. It revolved around a concert pianist who must steal priceless Fabergé eggs and deliver them to her fiancé's kidnappers as ransom. The early scenes were written for Hepburn at her current age of 57, which is what she preferred. But the producer decided the audience would appreciate only a younger Hepburn, and the part was rewritten for a younger character. Though she tried to be accommodating, her actions became stilted. Critics panned the film, and Young was quick to express regret and his belief that he had let Hepburn down.

The movie aired in February 1987 and received little attention. But acting had long before lost its place as a priority in Audrey's life; that had been replaced the moment Sean was born. Later that year, another development would launch her name back into the public spotlight and tug at her heartstrings for the rest of her life. In the fall of 1987, she and Robert were invited to attend the International Music Festival at Macao, which is located on the Chinese coast. Proceeds for the event were to benefit the United Nations Children's Fund (UNICEF), a nonprofit and nonpolitical group which works to help feed and clothe disadvantaged children from more than 160 nations as well as provide them with basics such as housing, health care, sanitation, and clean water.

Audrey spoke to the audience about her own childhood experiences and her gratitude toward the organization that eventually morphed into UNICEF immediately following World War II. The event struck a chord with Audrey, who quickly agreed to be the mistress of ceremonies for a concert by the World Philharmonic Orchestra in Tokyo that also raised money for UNICEF. UNICEF special events coordinator Christa Roth made all the arrangements and soon became her confidante and close friend. Audrey was a sensation in Japan, where the young girls had always followed the fashion trends she had set, but now also appreciated her charitable work. Roth was amazed and delighted at the positive effect Audrey had on the organization.

"She was so natural, relaxed and beautiful," Roth recalled. "It seemed inevitable that everyone would pay attention to her, and they did. She started by putting me at ease—there was nothing of the prima donna, nothing of the great movie star or fashion icon about her. She was just there to help a cause she believed in."[4]

Audrey believed in it enough to explore how she could further aid UNICEF. After all, her acting career was over. She had earned enough money to take care of her family for generations. Though marriage was no longer considered, she had finally found the man of her dreams in Robert, who never tried to dominate the relationship and whose brotherly friendship gave her more comfort in the company of a man than she had ever felt in her life. Sean was 27 and Luca was 17, and though she yearned to spend time with them, they were certainly no longer dependent on her. So it was time for Audrey to seek a new mission on which to concentrate her efforts. And after her trips to Macao and Tokyo, that mission became quite clear. She had always felt both sympathetic and empathetic toward both children and the underprivileged. What better way to help the causes of both than to work diligently and passionately with UNICEF?

The need was great. UNICEF was associated with the United Nations in name only; it received no funds from the worldwide organization. In the late 1980s, UNICEF was attempting to raise 20 million dollars to combat famine among five million people, half of whom were stricken in northern Ethiopia. Audrey threw herself into her work, as did fellow celebrities such as actors Peter Ustinov, Richard Attleborough, and Roger Moore, singer Julio Iglesias, and Sir Edmund Hillary, the first person to successfully scale Mt. Everest.

The addition of Audrey to the stable of volunteers was announced on March 8, 1988. She received nothing but a token payment of one dollar a year for her tireless work. In fact, she was forced to pay for all expenses, aside from travel and lodging. And such accommodations were hardly luxurious in third world countries. Disease was commonplace throughout many of the areas she visited, and the threat that she would contract one was always present and more than a bit frightening. Every trip was funded through public and private donation as well as charity events. Despite the fact that UNICEF was able to provide her so little, Audrey went through painstaking efforts to save the organization money. She kept track of every penny she spent in a notebook as a reminder to keep costs down. She flew only in coach in the belief that with people starving in the world, money should not be spent to place her in first class.

Audrey's insistence that Robert Wolders travel with her wherever she was assigned was quickly agreed on. Their first destination was indeed Ethiopia. She boarded a plane with just one carry-on bag and two suitcases—quite a light load for a world-renowned actor. The transportation following her flight was far from comfortable. She rode on rice sacks on the backs of trucks and in helicopters that hovered about the African plains. Audrey and Robert were dropped off in primitive villages that had no electricity, heat, or running water, though some were equipped with makeshift, ramshackle medical facilities.

But when she arrived, she expressed little concern for her own comfort. She cuddled with crying infants, shooing away flies that buzzed around their faces. She was horrified to see natives bathing and drinking from sewage-filled rivers. Audrey stood in stunned silence at an orphanage in northern Ethiopia and realized fully just how much she had to offer. "It's ironic that it was because of children that I stayed home all these years," she said. "Now it is for the sake of the children that I'm traveling all over the world."[5]

In one particularly poignant scene, Audrey asked an Ethiopian child who was standing by herself what she wanted to be when she grew up, whereupon the young child replied that she just hoped to be alive. Audrey felt the pain and hopelessness of the Ethiopian children, and her public utterances about their tragic lives came off as genuine. It wasn't always what she said, but the warmth and earnestness in which her words were spoken. And she was always prepared for her excursions.

"There were very, very, very few film stars who could match Audrey for total sincerity or discharge their duties without making you suspect they were in it for their own gain," Christa Roth said. "But Audrey, you see, did so much hard work—before, as well as after. She called for all the information we could supply her with about a particular crisis spot. She not only went on her mission well briefed, but she could speak of particular problems—not just UNICEF ones—with a detail that convinced her listeners that she had used her time well, and wasn't simply bringing back a sincere but rather superficial view of a country. She wanted, above all, to be credible."[6]

Audrey displayed the same professionalism in this unpaid task as she did performing in movies that paid her millions of dollars. And she felt more passionate about her current work. What angered her was that much of the starvation around the world was a result of war. She expressed on several occasions the need for educational institutions and international bodies to study ways for peace to be created. After all, the art of war had been studied and advanced throughout the centuries. The trip to Ethiopia, whose Marxist government actually criticized her after her visit, had made a profound impact on Audrey. And so did the knowledge that 250,000 children were dying every week around the world. "I have a broken heart," she said.

> I feel desperate. I can't stand the idea that two million people are in imminent danger of starving to death, many of them children, [and] not because there isn't tons of food sitting in the northern part of Shoa. It can't be distributed. Last spring, Red Cross and UNICEF workers were ordered out of the northern provinces because of two simultaneous civil wars....

> I went into rebel country and saw mothers and their children who had walked for ten days, even three weeks, looking for food, settling into the desert floor into makeshift camps where they may die. Horrible. That image is too much for me. The "Third World" is a term I don't like very much, because we're all one world. I want people to know that the largest part of humanity is suffering, that starvation exists even in a wealthy country like America—which is scandalous, a true disgrace.[7]

On her return from the war-torn African nation, she realized that only publicity could increase awareness of the problem. The same woman who fought for her privacy as an entertainer scheduled an exhausting number of press conferences with Robert's help. She flew around the globe from one major city to the next, speaking to the media in an attempt to get the word out and meeting with the leaders of nations, begging them to free up funds to stem the tide of starvation. On one trip to Washington, D.C., she did 15 press conferences and then successfully lobbied 25 members of Congress to add 60 million dollars in U.S. aid to Ethiopia.

Yet despite her whirlwind schedule and obvious sincerity as she traveled the world as an ambassador for UNICEF, the media were sometimes skeptical of her intentions. They pointed out the supposed contradiction that Audrey dressed in fabulous Givenchy fashions as she talked about her work, but the iconic actor simply replied that she felt she would be more effective in helping the children if she looked nice in front of the camera. And when one journalist spoke about how she was sacrificing her time, Audrey quickly argued that she was sacrificing nothing and that that could only be true if she was sacrificing something she wanted for something she didn't want. She replied that it was a gift to be given the opportunity to improve the lives of the children of the world.

"I was a little cynical about the setup at first," wrote one British journalist. "But as soon as Ms. Hepburn began speaking, all doubts fell away. Her commitment is passionate and sincere. She seemed near tears as she talked about 'the heart-rending and also heart-warming' sights she had seen in Ethiopia."[8]

In April 1989, Audrey began another journey to Africa, this time to the war-ravaged Sudan, where famine was widespread. Throwing caution to the wind, she traveled roads dotted with land mines and spoke with rebel leaders to loosen their stranglehold on the area to allow food and medicine to get through to those in most desperate need.

She was just getting started. She made 50 missions of mercy for UNICEF that year, including a wide range of trips to poor nations such as

El Salvador, Bangladesh, Guatemala, and Kenya. The camcorders rolled throughout each visit, showing Audrey sweetly cheering up both children and adults gripped by despair and hopelessness. She is seen feeding malnourished infants and walking fearlessly through battered and shredded corn stalks stripped of grain as gunfire is heard in the distance. She appears touched as native children in a classroom applaud her efforts. The videos of her excursions were again shown to the media and to national leaders on her return, as she pleaded for money. She spoke about the trillions or dollars spent on building militaries worldwide and the comparative pittance to save the lives of starving children.

The distress felt by those she visited, in particular, struck a chord with Audrey, who couldn't help but remember the final months of World War II, when she didn't know if she would live or die. She saw in the eyes of the children the same blankness of mind that war and hunger had brought to her nearly a half-century before. But rather than fill her with sadness and a sense of how little one woman could do, her work made her much happier and emotionally fulfilled than she had ever been during her acting career. She believed she was achieving something far more important than she ever could as an entertainer.

Audrey's spirits were also buoyed by Robert, to whom she grew closer by the day. He worked quietly behind the scenes when needed there and stood by her side when his presence was required. He played a major role in ensuring that all ran smoothly at her media appearances—from the sound quality of the microphones to the room quality at the hotels in which they were to stay. He listened thoughtfully and critiqued her speeches to make certain they sounded like they were indeed written by her. And when the subject of marriage came up, she would reply that a wedding ceremony could not strengthen the love and friendship she and Robert already enjoyed.

Undaunted by Audrey's obvious lack of desire to return to the silver screen, filmmakers continued to send scripts her way. The idea of taking on a major role was far from her thoughts, more so now that she had embraced her tasks for UNICEF, but one opportunity did catch her attention because it related well to her current work. She accepted a bit part in a film titled *Always,* which was to be directed by the esteemed Steven Spielberg. The movie was about a wartime flyer (played by Richard Dreyfuss) who was killed in battle, then returned to earth as an angel whose mission was to guide his fiancée into love and marriage with her newfound boyfriend.

Hepburn's cameo appearance was as an angel who welcomes the flyer to heaven. Though one might wonder why Spielberg wanted to spend more than a million dollars to lure a legendary star to such a small role, he believed the angel in question required the mythical, heavenly qualities Hepburn had in abundance. And quite selflessly, she turned over much of that money to UNICEF.

In the movie, the angel played by Hepburn informs the fallen flyer that he is indeed in heaven and prepares him for his earthly tasks. Her last line is symbolic of what she felt her calling to be in real life. She instructs the fighter pilot to use his spirit not for selfish gain, but rather to help others. It would be the last movie line she would ever utter.

By fighting for the lives of children desperate for attention, Hepburn was also taking a political stand. After all, she argued, alleviating such blights as hunger and sickness among the world's young required little money in comparison to what was being spent in preparation for war. The United Nations had created the idea of a development fund in which nations would spend 1 percent of their annual budgets to provide for those in the direst need. Hepburn spearheaded the charge to convince the world community to accept the challenge.

"Less than one-half of one percent of today's world economy would be the total required to alleviate the worst aspects of poverty and would meet basic human needs for the next ten years," she told the U.S. House of Representatives. "We cannot ignore the economic issues that have made the 1980s into a decade of despair.... The heaviest burden of a decade of frenzied borrowing is falling not on the military nor on those foreign bank accounts nor on those who conceived the years of waste, but on the poor who are having to do without the bare necessities.... When the impact becomes visible in the rising death rates of children, then what has happened is simply an outrage against a large section of humanity. Nothing can justify it."[9]

Hepburn went on to explain that only 5 dollars were needed to vaccinate a child for life, a paltry 6 cents were required to keep that same child hydrated for a year, and 84 cents would prevent him or her from going blind. She chastised the congresspeople and other world leaders for allowing so much money to be spent on weaponry created to kill others and so little on keeping children alive.

## NOTES

1. Barry Paris, *Audrey Hepburn* (New York: G. P. Putnam's Sons, 1996), 287.

2. Donald Spoto, *Enchantment: The Life of Audrey Hepburn* (New York: Harmony Books, 2006), 287–88.

3. Paris, *Audrey Hepburn*, 297.

4. Spoto, *Enchantment*, 291.

5. Alexander Walker, *Audrey: Her Real Story* (New York: St. Martin's Griffin, 1994), 264.

6. Ibid., 265.

7. Quoted in Glenn Plaskin, *US Magazine*, October 17, 1988.

8. Lynn Barber, "Hepburn's Relief," *London Sunday Express*, May 1, 1988.

9. Audrey Hepburn at a hearing of the Select Committee on Hunger, House of Representatives, Washington, D.C., April 6, 1989.

# Chapter 11

# WORKING HERSELF TO DEATH

Those close to Hepburn during the late 1980s and early 1990s felt little doubt that her travel schedule for the United Nations Children's Fund (UNICEF) was taking a toll on her. They suggested and sometimes begged her to slow down, but to no avail. She was on a mission, and not even physical deterioration could prevent her from working toward the betterment of others.

Hepburn could have chosen to ease up on both the number of trips and the number of stops on her itineraries. On her arrival in one country, she saw 20 children who had died the previous night of starvation and illness being loaded onto a truck. She nearly swooned at the horrific sight but recovered to spend time with other children who would also soon be dead. The overwhelming grief she felt was soon overtaken by the understanding that she had work to do. She knew it was up to her to tell the world what was happening in even the most remote, primitive spots on the globe. Hepburn was driven. She simply refused to relax even when her body was begging for it. She tossed and turned at night, managing little sleep with her thoughts on the enormity of her task and the suffering of the people with whom she worked. And despite all the warnings from the medical community, she continued to chain smoke. UNICEF field officer Ian Mac-Leod expressed his dismay at watching her hands shake uncontrollably.

Hepburn did take a respite from her fieldwork in May 1991, but only in a continued effort to help the cause. She traveled to England to meet composer and London Symphony Orchestra conductor Michael Tilson Thomas, who had set the words to the diary of Anne Frank to music and performed it while Hepburn served as narrator in a concert that raised

money for UNICEF. It was a personal triumph, considering she had refused to portray Anne Frank in any play or movie because of her overwhelming feelings of empathy for the teenage girl who was eventually
murdered by the Nazis. She was finally able to participate in a project that
utilized the diary of Anne Frank in a meaningful and beneficial way. The
event raised about 60,000 dollars for the charity.

Every stop offered new circumstances and challenges. Hepburn always
took the time to learn about the specific maladies that plagued each nation
so she could speak about them intelligently to its representatives and to the
outside world. But the children neither knew nor cared about the political
and geographical reasons for their plight. Hepburn saw the same emptiness
and misery in the eyes of the children of Bangladesh as those of Somalia or
El Salvador. Whether it was war or flooding or drought that caused such
tremendous problems mattered not a bit to the children. Hepburn's task
when she met with the children was the same no matter which country
she was visiting. And that was to make their lives brighter, even if just
for one fleeting moment. Taking steps to improve their lives permanently
would have to wait for when she met with the national leaders.

Unfortunately, the efforts that were needed to accomplish her goals
were politically based. But the fall of Communism in the early 1990s,
which virtually ended the cold war, allowed governments to free money
for humanitarian causes. By 1990, Hepburn proudly announced in Rome
that UNICEF and the World Health Organization had achieved univer-
sal child immunization, which meant that 80 percent of the world's one-
year-olds had been immunized against the six diseases most responsible
for childhood deaths. That figure was 5 percent just 16 years earlier. The
immunization program had been quite ambitious. But many Americans
were alarmed to know that immunizations against childhood diseases in
their own country were actually decreasing. She offered that in cities such
as Houston and Miami, the percentage of children who were immunized
was under that of North Africa. And she added her view that poverty in
America was clearly a major problem.

When CBS This Morning host Howard K. Smith brought up the notion
of Americans taking care of Americans first, however, Hepburn was prepared. "I think we can do both," she said. "Sure, we take care of our own
children first. Charity begins at home. But there's no reason why we can't
have love or time or money or food for children in Africa."[1]

Two days later, she sounded a similar refrain on Larry King Live. "It's
the endless wars that have destroyed what we've tried to do [in Africa],"
she added. "Adults fight and children die. Peace is what I'm pleading for,
because until there's peace we won't be able to construct."[2]

That same year, Hepburn co hosted the "Concert for Peace" in Oslo, Norway, which was attended by such former and current world leaders as Jimmy Carter, Francois Mitterand, and Nelson Mandela. And in 1991, she was invited back to Washington by senators Philip Leahy of Vermont and Nancy Kassebaum of Kansas to make another plea to Washington congresspeople for increased financial aid to Africa. Kassebaum spoke admiringly of Hepburn's commitment to the suffering children of the world and actually planned on meeting the iconic celebrity in Africa, but convenient arrangements couldn't be finalized.

By that time, Hepburn had become the most effective ambassador UNICEF had ever known. Not only did she work tirelessly in the field, but her background as an actor also made her a convincing orator. She mixed passion with a sense of realism in speaking to national leaders. She attempted to sway those in power to loosen the purse strings through what she believed strongly to be morally right. Her power of persuasion was particularly evident in a speech she made to members of the United Nations, when she countered arguments made against her efforts:

> The human brain and body are formed within the first five years of life, and there is no second chance. It is the young child whose individual development today, and whose social contribution tomorrow, are being shaped by the economics of now. It is the young child who is paying the highest of all prices. We cannot therefore ignore the economic issues, which for so many millions of the world's poorest families have made the 1980s into a decade of despair.
>
> ...I must admit to you that the magnitude of the task that UNICEF has undertaken sometimes overwhelms me, and I am saddened and frustrated when I stop to think of what we cannot do—like change the world overnight—or when I have to deal with the cynics of this world who argue, is it morally right to save the lives of children who will only grow up to more suffering and poverty due to overpopulation? Letting children die is not the remedy to overpopulation; family planning and birth spacing is. Rapid population growth can be slowed by giving the world's poor a better life, giving them health, education, housing, nutrition, civil rights.
>
> ...Today I speak for those children who cannot speak for themselves: children who are going blind through lack of vitamins; children who are slowly being mutilated by polio; children who are wasting away in so many ways through lack of

water; for the estimated one hundred million street children
in this world who have no choice but to leave home in order
to survive, who have absolutely nothing but their courage and
their smiles and their dreams....The task that lies ahead for
UNICEF is ever greater, whether it be repatriating millions of
children in Afghanistan or teaching children how to play who
have only learned how to kill.[3]

The following year she made an historic excursion to Vietnam. It has
been speculated that the trip received little attention in the United States
because the United States had fought an unpopular and unsuccessful war
there in the 1960s and early 1970s, in an attempt to prevent North Vietnamese insurgents from spreading Communism into South Vietnam.
Hepburn didn't care that Americans had no stomach for reopening its
wounds from a controversial historical period. She was apolitical, and the
Vietnamese children needed her help. Though starvation was not a major
issue in Vietnam, its children were still being affected by a war that had
raged in that country for a quarter century. She was greeted lovingly by
the Vietnamese, including General Vo Nguyen Giap, the deputy prime
minister whose military skills played a major role in defeating the American and South Vietnamese armies of the previous generation.

The trip to Communist Vietnam didn't deter U.S. president George
Bush from presenting Hepburn in 1991 with the Presidential Medal of
Freedom, the highest honor that he could bestow on an individual.

It also served as a precursor to her most heart-wrenching tour, that of
Somalia in 1992. Hepburn had planned to visit the people of the war-torn
and poverty-stricken African nation a year earlier, but other assignments
had been deemed more important, and Somalia was considered unsafe at
the time. She finally arrived in September and was taken aback by the
devastation. She had witnessed helplessness and despair in every country
to which she had traveled as a UNICEF representative, but she had seen
nothing that braced her for what she would encounter in Somalia. Mass
graves peppered the landscape. They awaited others who had been displaced by war and were simply waiting to join the rotting corpses. Thousands of children cried to be fed, but to no avail.

On her arrival, Hepburn watched as about 100 dead children were
loaded onto a truck. Many of those still alive had been badly ravaged by
the civil war that had claimed the lives of their families and even entire
villages. There was nary a road on which to bring food if it was available. Sanitation was nonexistent. So was any form of government. The
crops and cattle were dead. Widespread looting had eliminated anything

of value in the area. Anarchy ruled the day. It was the children who were suffering the most.

"I walked right into a nightmare," Hepburn recalled. "Ethiopia had been brutally bad, but Somalia was beyond belief. No stories in the press could prepare me for what I saw. The unspeakable agony of it! I kept seeing these countless little, fragile, emaciated children sitting under the trees, waiting to be fed. There wasn't food, yet they waited. Most of them were very ill—dying, I guess. I'll never forget their huge eyes in tiny faces and the terrible silence."[4]

Hepburn's trip brought badly needed attention to the plight of Somalia. Soon food was arriving under the watchful eye and protection of United Nations peacekeepers and the U.S. Navy. She was visibly touched when a group of sailors and marines aboard the USS *Tarawa* aircraft carrier, who had been informed of the charitable efforts just an hour earlier, handed her a check for 4,000 dollars. Media attention that had been lacking during her trip to Vietnam increased considerably. American cable news network CNN joined forces with other media outlets throughout the world to provide daily coverage of the horrors of war and famine that had devastated the African nation.

The result was swift and effective. President Bush, who was serving his final days in the White House, sent thousands of American troops to Somalia to curb the violence, transform the anarchy into order and calm, and provide food for those most in need. Mass starvation was quelled. What proved most encouraging to Hepburn and much of the world was that the military had been utilized in a strictly humanitarian effort.

Hepburn was exhausted on returning from the four-day mission that included a stop in Kenya to visit refugee camps, and it showed. Photos taken of Hepburn during the excursion showed that a woman who had always been painfully thin now looked downright emaciated and more than a bit haggard. She seemed to have aged 10 years since taking on her responsibilities with UNICEF. Her facial expressions displayed through film reels were ones of sullen determination. Her sunken, shadowy eyes looked as if they had not been shut in restful slumber for weeks. Nevertheless, she was determined to continue.

Local doctors were summoned when Hepburn experienced spasmodic attacks to her lower stomach during her second day in Somalia. The lack of modern technology in the area precluded any thorough diagnosis, but local doctors believed she might have been suffering from amoebic dysentery and suggested strongly that she at least temporarily halt her activities. Hepburn dismissed the notion and insisted that this was no time to rest. Rather than take the medical advice, she tried to soothe her pain by rubbing her stomach and trying to convince herself that the discomfort was merely a product of distress.

On her return to Europe for a period of rest and a post-trip briefing, she again refused to check into a hospital. She even kept her appointment several days later to address the Foreign Press Association in London. She and Robert were soon headed for Rochester, New York, where she was to be presented with an award from the George Eastman House, which followed a screening of *Breakfast at Tiffany's*. Though in pain, she answered a series of questions from the media and the public and even apologized to one fan who chastised her for leaving an event early the night before, claiming it was a result of jet lag.

"She didn't want to say, 'I'm also in great pain,'" Wolders said. "Nobody knew how ill she was—how could they? I didn't, either. It was quite heroic what she did that night. They never had such a turnout and couldn't accommodate everyone in the [Dryden] Theater. They had to use the ballroom, with a closed-circuit TV, and Audrey made it a point at the end to go to the other hall and greet the people there as well."[5]

Soon, however, the pain reached a level even Audrey couldn't ignore. Though hesitant to check in to a hospital, she at least agreed to be examined at Cedars Sinai Medical Center in Los Angeles in mid-October 1992. The initial plan was outpatient treatment, but tests and X-rays revealed a tumor of the colon and the necessity of an operation to determine if it was malignant.

An emergency surgery to remove the tumor was performed on November 1. A partial reconstruction of the colon was also done, after which she was admitted to the intensive care unit of the hospital for further testing. The prognosis was quickly deemed positive. The tumor was given a low-grade malignancy rating, which led medical personnel to announce their belief that it had been nipped in the bud. Audrey was given permission to walk around her private suite and accept visitors; friends Gregory Peck and Elizabeth Taylor were among them. Though more tests were in the offing, Audrey and her friends felt a tremendous sense of relief.

That hopefulness would soon dissipate. Three weeks later, Audrey began feeling severe stomach pains and was hurried back to the hospital. This time the tests showed an acute intestinal blockage. Moreover, doctors feared that the malignant tumor had spread. The news continued to worsen. Two weeks before Christmas, she was told that she would have only three months to live.

It was then that Robert's essential love and friendship became even more appreciated. He remained at Audrey's bedside throughout her stay in the hospital, as only her close friends from the entertainment world were allowed to visit. There was little conversation or fond remembrance—she was drugged to lessen her pain and sleeping most of the time. It was at that time she was heartened by word of American troops landing in Somalia, but it was ironic that while the peacekeepers were saving lives, she herself was slipping away. The news did strengthen her conviction that her work had not been in vain, and the word of her own physical deterioration generated greater coverage of her work with UNICEF and the goals that still needed to be accomplished.

The media certainly didn't focus solely on Audrey's charitable contributions. Newspapers, magazines, and television reports glorified her movie career. Though quite a flattering spotlight was placed on her, it couldn't be denied that such attention could be construed as the obituary of a woman who was still alive. Famed British writer and critic Sheridan Morley spoke of the uneasiness he felt during one particular trip to New York City as he noticed a video store preparing their Hepburn tribute on her passing. "[I noticed its windows] stacked from floor to ceiling [with] boxes and boxes of her films already neatly arranged as some kind of memorial tribute, the way that photographs of mortally ill or nearly deceased or newly deceased royalty used to be placed in the windows of Viennese pastry shops," he said. "Struck at first by what seemed to me to be appalling taste, I stood in the rain to stare at the videos and realized that it was in fact a wonderful celebration of a great career."[6]

That career, however, had always taken a backseat to her personal life and, in the end, her commitment to the suffering children of the world. Her priorities were never more evident than in the weeks after she was informed that her illness was terminal, when she hightailed it out of Los Angeles and flew to her beloved Switzerland. She was too weak to fly on a commercial jetliner. Socialite and philanthropist Bunny Mellon, who worked with Audrey's friend and fashion designer Hubert de Givenchy, arranged to have a private jet, complete with doctor and nurse, take Audrey home.

Audrey arrived on December 21, looking frail and weak and holding tightly on to Robert as they descended the steps of the jet. The housekeeper and two Jack Russell terriers greeted the couple, then Sean met them in their home, which had been filled with flowers sent by well-wishers. Audrey refused to remain bedridden. She rested in the morning, ate light meals, and took occasional walks when the weather wasn't particularly cold. And after she celebrated the holidays with Robert and her family, she told everyone it had been the best Christmas of her life.

The end, however, was near. While Audrey awaited the inevitable in her Swiss home, the world paid tribute to her life and career. The Screen

Actors Guild of America presented in her name the Life Achievement Award, which was accepted by rising young actor Julia Roberts. Roberts read to the audience Hepburn's last public statement, one that expressed in her typically humble style her appreciation for the business that gave her a livelihood, despite the fact that it had caused her so many moments of uncertainty and anxiousness:

> As a child I was taught that it was bad manners to draw attention to yourself and make a spectacle of yourself. I then went on to make a rather nice living doing just that—with a little help from the greatest directors, the best writers, the most fabulous stars, glorious photography, terrific scores, super clothes, and the best crews in the industry. My job was to be on time and know my lines. [Others] helped and honed, triggered and taught, pushed and pulled...guided and nurtured a totally unknown, insecure, inexperienced, skinny broad into a marketable commodity. I am proud to have been in a business that gives pleasure, creates beauty and awakens our conscience, arouses compassion and perhaps most importantly, gives millions a respite from our so violent world.[7]

It was also announced that she would receive a humanitarian award for her UNICEF work, but that would be presented at the Oscars in March. Sadly, Audrey doubted that she would be alive to see the honor.

On January 10, Audrey strolled around her garden for the last time. She yearned to spend a few final moments in one of her most serene and cherished settings. She stopped at each plot and reminded Robert what kind of care that particular plant required. During those final weeks, she often urged the man who many thought she would marry to smile for her. Robert was in no smiling mood, but he forced them on his face for her.

By mid-January, whatever strength she had left began to drain away. Word of her impending passing was spread around the world. Mother Teresa of Calcutta led a 24-hour prayer vigil for Audrey, who by that time was considering marrying Robert as a show of love and appreciation. But it was for just those reasons she decided against it. "No, Robbie, it's not necessary," she told him. "You're closer than any husband."[8]

Though Audrey understood that she was on the brink of death, her spirits remained upbeat. And at seven o'clock on the evening of January 20, 1993, she passed away in her home. The word of her death reached the other townspeople and shop owners, many of whom placed candles in their windows. Soon the bell at the nearby Protestant church tolled in honor of one of the world's most iconic and beloved figures. And after she had passed, the words she had once spoken to London journalist David Lewin were remembered. They would be heartening words that assured one and all that she died with no regrets and only contentment in her heart: "If my world were to cave in tomorrow," she had told Lewin, "I would look back on all the pleasures, excitements and worthwhileness I have been lucky enough to have had. Not the sadnesses, miscarriages, or my father leaving home, but the joy of everything else. It will have been enough."[9]

## NOTES

1. Audrey Hepburn to Harry K. Smith on CBS *This Morning*, June 3, 1991.

2. Audrey Hepburn to Larry King on *Larry King Live*, June 5, 1991.

3. Audrey Hepburn to members of the United Nations staff at the invitation of the "1 Percent for Development Fund," June 13, 1989.

4. Diana Maychick, *Audrey Hepburn: An Intimate Portrait* (New York: Carol, 1993), 233.

5. Barry Paris, *Audrey Hepburn* (New York: G. P. Putnam's Sons, 1996), 358.

6. Alexander Walker, *Audrey: Her Real Story* (New York: St. Martin's Griffin, 1994), 279.

7. Paris, *Audrey Hepburn*, 366.

8. Walker, *Audrey*, 281.

9. Ibid.

# EPILOGUE

It didn't seem to matter that Audrey passed away on the day of President Bill Clinton's inauguration. Her death dominated the news as well as the memories of all whom she had touched. Condolences poured in from throughout the world.

Among the most affected was the United Nations Children's Fund (UNICEF) executive Christa Roth, who had convinced herself that Audrey would survive. The British Broadcasting Corporation had asked Roth to record an obituary, but she refused in a vain hope that the woman who had brought her organization to prominence would pull through. In the end, however, she and UNICEF would suffer.

Yet Roth didn't focus on Audrey's work for UNICEF when the time finally came to express her thoughts about the iconic figure; rather, she spoke about Audrey's innate ability to relate to others. "I would have asked Audrey's advice on any matter, however personal to me," Roth said. "She had that rare capacity to listen to people and to come up with the right advice, by instinct as much as anything. She gave you her whole attention. Some people you miss."[1]

One might believe that all the condolences received at the UNICEF offices could not realistically be read. But Sean Ferrer indeed devoured one and all and even replied with words of thanks to most of them, particularly those from people who had also worked to give hope to those suffering in third world countries.

Though the diagnosis of colon cancer gave the world a chance to brace for it, Audrey's death still came as quite a shock to friends. They looked at her as a saint who deserved a long and fruitful life, though Audrey never considered herself saintly. Among those who were stunned was fellow actor Arlene Dahl, who said, "You looked at her, and all you could think was that nothing bad should ever happen to her." Added Shirley MacLaine, who costarred with Audrey in *The Children's Hour*, "If there was a cross between the salt of the earth and a regal queen, then she was it."[2] World-renowned stars such as Gregory Peck, Sophia Loren, Sean Connery, and Alan Arkin also chimed in, but perhaps Elizabeth Taylor's succinct statement expressed it best: "God has a most beautiful new angel now."[3]

Director Billy Wilder believed Hepburn's death signaled an end of an era in the movie industry. He believed that unique quality was evident both on and off the screen, one that he noticed after Hepburn won her best actress Oscar for *Roman Holiday*. Wilder said,

> She was not high-falutin. She did not play "The Oscar Winner." She was humble. She listened intelligently. She made what she said and felt so true that her partner—whether it was Holden or Bogart or Cooper—had to react the proper way.... Audrey was known for something which has disappeared, and that is elegance, grace and manners—things you cannot take a course in. You're born with it or not. What is needed to really become a star is an extra element that God gives or doesn't give you. You cannot learn it. She just was blessed. God kissed her on the cheek, and there she was.[4]

The funeral was held on January 24, with the ceremony at Eglise de Tolochenaz, a simple stone church in her village. The town had banned Sunday funerals but made an exception for this one as mourners poured in from all over the world and another 600 townspeople lined the streets to listen to the service, which was performed by 83-year-old pastor Maurice Eindiguer, who had wed Audrey and Mel in 1954, baptized Sean six years later, and given Audrey her last rites just two hours before she died. Those attending included first husband Mel Ferrer and his fourth wife. Mel struggled to hold back his tears as he embraced Sean. It wasn't Mel's first emotional encounter in recent days. He saw Audrey on her deathbed, touched her hand and kissed her forehead. It was the first time he had laid eyes on his first wife since Sean's wedding 10 years earlier.

Sean would have many good days thereafter, but certainly those leading up to and following his mother's death were not among them. But he took with him the comforting knowledge that she left with no regrets and died in her sleep. And he felt the goodness she brought to others in his heart long after she passed away.

"Mummy believed in one thing above all: She believed in love," he wrote in his biography. "She believed love could heal, fix, mend and make everything fine and good in the end...and it did."[5]

Three months after Hepburn's death, the Audrey Hepburn Memorial Tribute held a concert to benefit the Audrey Hepburn Memorial Fund at the United Nations. The event, which featured many of the world's most prestigious musicians and actors, gathered to pay homage to her charitable work. A 15-minute film spotlighting that work highlighted the evening activities.

The attendees included not only a number of classical music greats, but stars of the entertainment world such as Barbara Walters, Roger Moore, and Harry Belafonte. United Nations secretary-general Boutros-Boutros Ghali delivered a speech in which he praised Audrey for her selflessness during her time working with UNICEF. "She modestly denied giving much," he said. "On the contrary, she told us again and again that she was the one on the receiving end, and how the courage and dignity of the children and the mothers strengthened and uplifted her."[6]

Audrey searched her entire life for happiness and fulfillment, and she finally found it in her last years by bringing smiles to the faces of battered, hapless souls. She found it in the simplicity of puttering around her garden. She found it in a man who was too much of a friend to marry. But find it she did, finally.

## NOTES

1. Alexander Walker, *Audrey: Her Real Story* (New York: St. Martin's Griffin, 1994), 282.

2. Susan Schindehette, "Our Fair Lady," *People Weekly* 39 (1993): 60.

3. Walker, *Audrey,* 283.

4. Billy Wilder in *Audrey Hepburn Remembered,* video documentary (Los Angeles: Wombat Productions, 1994).

5. Sean Hepburn Ferrer, *Audrey Hepburn: An Elegant Spirit* (New York: Atria Books, 2003), 217.

6. UNICEF, "Memorial Tribute to Audrey Hepburn," April 27, 1993, http://www.hepburntribute.com/tribute.html.

# Appendix

# WORKS OF STAGE AND SCREEN

### FILMOGRAPHY

*Dutch in Seven Lessons* (1948). Played an unnamed KLM airline stewardess in an informational film.

*One Wild Oat* (1951). Played an unnamed hotel receptionist.

*Laughter in Paradise* (1951). Briefly played an unnamed cigarette girl in a nightclub.

*The Lavender Hill Mob* (1951). Played a cigarette girl Chiquita.

*Young Wives' Tale* (1951). Played Eve Lester, a guest in the home of fighting couples.

*The Secret People* (1952). Played Nora, a ballet dancer involved unwittingly in an assassination plot.

*We Go to Monte Carlo* (1952). Played film star Linda Farrel.

*Roman Holiday* (1953). First major role. Played Anya Smith, a runaway princess in Rome. Won an Academy Award for Best Actress. Won a Golden Globe for Best Drama Actress.

*Sabrina* (1954). Played Sabrina, a chauffeur's daughter who falls in love with the two sons of a millionaire. Nominated for an Academy Award for Best Actress.

*War and Peace* (1956). Played heroine Natasha Rostov in an adaptation of the Tolstoy classic. Nominated for a Golden Globe for Best Drama Actress.

*Funny Face* (1957). Played Jo Stockton, a bookshop assistant transformed into a star by a fashion photographer.

*Love in the Afternoon* (1957). Played Ariane Chavasse, a detective's daughter romanced by a millionaire ladies' man. Nominated for a Golden Globe for Best Musical/Comedy Actress.

*Green Mansions* (1959). Played nature girl Rima.

*The Nun's Story* (1959). Played Sister Luke, a nun doubling as a nurse in Belgian Congo. Nominated for an Academy Award for Best Actress. Nominated for a Golden Globe for Best Drama Actress.

*The Unforgiven* (1960). Played a Native American girl, Rachel Zachary, living with a white family in Texas.

*Breakfast at Tiffany's* (1961). Played Holly Golightly. Nominated for an Academy Award for Best Actress.

*The Children's Hour* (1962). Played Karen Wright, a schoolteacher accused of lesbianism.

*Charade* (1963). Played Regina Lambert, a widow involved in international intrigue.

*Paris When It Sizzles* (1964). Played screenwriter's assistant Gabrielle Simpson.

*My Fair Lady* (1964). Played Eliza Doolittle, a Cockney flower girl transformed into a sophisticated lady by a man with whom she eventually falls in love. Nominated for a Golden Globe for Best Musical/Comedy Actress.

*How to Steal a Million* (1966). Played the daughter of art forger Nicole Bonnet.

*Two for the Road* (1967). Played Joanna Wallace, a young woman experiencing marital problems. Nominated for a Golden Globe for Best Musical/Comedy Actress.

*Wait until Dark* (1967). Played Suzy Hendrix, a blind woman terrorized by drug dealers. Nominated for an Academy Award for Best Actress. Nominated for a Golden Globe for Best Drama Actress.

*Robin and Marian* (1976). Played middle-aged Marian in a fast-forwarded Robin Hood adaptation.

*Bloodline* (1979). Played Elizabeth Roffe, a pharmaceutical heiress threatened by a murderer.

*They All Laughed* (1982). Played Angela Niotes, an estranged wife of multimillionaire who falls for a detective.

*Always* (1989). Briefly played Hap, an angel in heaven.

## THEATRICAL PRODUCTIONS

*High Button Shoes* (1949). Unnamed chorus girl in a musical.

*Sauce Tartare* (1949). Unnamed chorus girl in a musical.

*Sauce Piquante* (1950). Featured player in a musical.

*Gigi* (1951). Played Gigi, a young Parisian trained by her grandmother and aunt about finer things in life. Won the 1952 Theater World Award.

*Ondine* (1954). Played a water nymph named Ondine. Won a Tony Award for Best Actress.

*Mayerling* (1957). Played a baroness named Marie Vetsera.

**TELEVISION**

*Love among Thieves* (1987). Played baroness Caroline DuLac in a TV movie.

*Gardens of the World with Audrey Hepburn* (1993). Played herself in a Public Broadcasting Service miniseries. Won an Emmy for Outstanding Individual Achievement for Informational Programming.

# SELECTED BIBLIOGRAPHY

Ferrer, Sean Hepburn. *Audrey Hepburn: An Elegant Spirit*. New York: Atria Books, 2003.

Higham, Charles. *Audrey: The Life of Audrey Hepburn*. New York: Macmillan, 1984.

Maychick, Diana. *Audrey Hepburn: An Intimate Portrait*. New York: Carol, 1993.

Paris, Barry. *Audrey Hepburn*. New York: G. P. Putnam's Sons, 1996.

Spoto, Donald. *Enchantment: The Life of Audrey Hepburn*. New York: Harmony Books, 2006.

Walker, Alexander. *Audrey: Her Real Story*. New York: St. Martin's Griffin, 1994.

# INDEX

## About the Author

MARTIN GITLIN is a freelance book writer and journalist based in Cleveland, Ohio. In addition to *Diana, Princess of Wales* (Greenwood 2008), he has written several history books for students, including works on the landmark *Brown v. Board of Education* case, Battle of The Little Bighorn and the Stock Market Crash of 1929. He has also written biographies of NASCAR drivers Jimmie Johnson and Jeff Gordon. Gitlin worked for two decades as a sportswriter, during which time he won more than 45 awards, including first place for general excellence from the Associated Press. That organization also selected him as one of the top four feature writers in Ohio.